NEOT KEDUMIM
THE BIBLICAL LANDSCAPE RESERVE IN ISRAEL

Artwork: Ada Bahat, Amir Publishing Co. Ltd.

Tree and Shrub in Our Biblical Heritage

Nogah Hareuveni

Translated from Hebrew and adapted
by Helen Frenkley

Neot Kedumim Ltd.
Kiryat Ono, Israel

All photographs are by Nogah Hareuveni
except the following:
Helen Frenkley: 4, 49 (upper and bottom right),
52 (upper left), 54, 55, 82, 95, 106 (upper left),
120 (upper left and right)
Ma'ayan Hareuveni: 81 (right)
Ruth (Narkiss) Precker: 57 (bottom and right), 105
Unknown: 13

The credits that appear above
are hereby made a part of this copyright page.
Copyright © 1984 by Neot Kedumim Ltd.,
P.O.Box 299, Kiryat Ono, Israel.

ISBN 965-233-011-6

Typeset by Otiot Dfuss Ltd., Tel Aviv
Color separation by Scanli Ltd., Tel Aviv
Plates and printing by Peli Printing Works Ltd., Givatayim
Printed in Israel
Second Printing – 1989

p. 3

"There is hope for a tree."
*Many hundreds of years old, this olive tree,
threatened with destruction on its original site,
now thrives in its new home at Neot Kedumim.*

p. 4

**"Ascent of the Four Species of Sukkot" at Neot
Kedumim:** *three of the Talmudic candidates for
the "leafy tree."*

p. 9

"How pleasing is this furrow!"

p. 10

"How pleasing is this tree!"

כִּי יֵשׁ לָעֵץ תִּקְוָה אִם־יִכָּרֵת וְעוֹד יַחֲלִיף וְיֹנַקְתּוֹ לֹא תֶחְדָּל
אִם־יַזְקִין בָּאָרֶץ שָׁרְשׁוֹ וּבֶעָפָר יָמוּת גִּזְעוֹ
מֵרֵיחַ מַיִם יַפְרִחַ וְעָשָׂה קָצִיר כְּמוֹ־נָטַע (איוב י"ד ז-ט)

"THERE IS HOPE FOR A TREE. IF IT BE CUT DOWN IT WILL SPROUT AGAIN AND FRESH SHOOTS WILL NOT
FAIL THOUGH ITS ROOTS GROW OLD IN THE EARTH AND THE STUMP IS DYING IN THE GROUND. IF
IT SCENTS WATER IT MAY BREAK INTO BUD AND MAKE NEW GROWTH LIKE A YOUNG PLANT." (Job 14:7-9)

To Martin Abelove, who once again made it all possible

ALL PROCEEDS BENEFIT NEOT KEDUMIM - THE BIBLICAL LANDSCAPE RESERVE IN ISRAEL

TABLE OF CONTENTS

MAIN TEXT

SUPPLEMENTARY TEXT

Translator's Note

Translating a book of this kind poses special problems. Not only is the material complex, but it calls for a fair knowledge of botanical, biblical and Talmudic terminology. Since we hope this book will find its way into the hands of the casual reader, scholar and layman, Jewish and non-Jewish, I have endeavored to help the English reader through some of the thornier thickets by providing explanatory notes not included in the original Hebrew text.

In translating the Hebrew Bible into English, I primarily relied upon *The Jerusalem Bible* (Koren Publishers, Jerusalem, 1983), *The New English Bible* (Oxford University Press, New York, 1971), and *Torah, Prophets, Writings* (Jewish Publication Society of America, Philadelphia, 1962, 1978, 1982 respectively). In numerous instances, however, I have used these translations only as the framework within which I have rendered the more accurate understanding suggested by Nogah Hareuveni. As in *Nature in Our Biblical Heritage*, I have chosen clarity rather than literal precision. **All biblical quotations are identified according to the chapter and verse numbers of the Hebrew Bible.**

Spelling of biblical names presented a serious problem. With the notable exception of *The Jerusalem Bible*, the transliterations first used in the *King James* version continue to be used in almost all English translations, whether or not these spellings reflect the correct pronunciation of the Hebrew name. For the sake of clarity and accessibility, I have used the common English transliterations thoughout, **except** where a more correct transliteration is crucial to the understanding of the linguistic root of the name, e.g. Avi-melekh (Abimelech) (see p.59), Tzlofkhad (Zelophehad) (see p.45). Names of Sages are spelled according to the *Encyclopaedia Judaica* to enable the reader to refer to that source for additional information.

Some Mishnaic and Talmudic quotations were rendered as in the *Hebrew-English Edition of the Babylonian Talmud* (Traditional Press, New York, 1980); however, quotations from the midrashim, the Jerusalem Talmud, and all quotations from the Order of Seeds *(Seder Zra'im)* in the Mishna were rendered into English by this translator.

The accepted conventions are used to indicate quotations from the Mishna (name of the tractate, followed by chapter and paragraph number), the Babylonian Talmud (name of the tractate, number of the leaf, followed by "a" or "b" to indicate the page side that is standard to all editions of the Babylonian Talmud), and the Jerusalem Talmud (always indicated as "Jerusalem Talmud," followed by the tractate, chapter, and paragraph number).

Throughout the book, the reader will note that the italicized Hebrew names of plants are widely used. This is to **lessen** the confusion caused by using misleading English common names that are sometimes unfamiliar to the reader. I hope the reader will overcome the initial inconvenience, will quickly become familiar with the Hebrew names, and will agree that they serve to clarify hitherto obscure texts and incorrect identifications.

I have employed the standard Jewish usage of BCE, "before the common era," for B.C., and CE, "common era," instead of A.D.

Definitions of a number of basic terms and brief information about each of the Sages mentioned in this book are listed in chronological order in the appendix. The number in parentheses [1] indicates an appendix reference.

Helen Frenkley

To the Reader

If you have skimmed through this book and are interested in reading the text, please take time to read the following as well.

This book contains diverse information on a relatively small number of Israel's trees and shrubs: descriptions, uses, and their rich didactic role in Jewish tradition. This is an adventure in the creative rediscovery of the fusion of nature in the land of Israel with the traditions of the Jewish people.

This book does not even begin to survey all available information about these plants, nor does the book incorporate all the biblical verses and comments of the Sages [5] relating to these plants.

The purpose of this book is to engage the reader's interest in specific subjects that, as far as I know, have not been dealt with by other writers or commentators from the particular points of view emphasized here.

My involvement with this subject matter, as well as the methodology used in seeking answers to the questions raised, began with my parents and teachers, **Dr. Ephraim and Hannah Hareuveni**. They were the first modern botanists to establish new methods for the study of nature and landscape in Jewish tradition. Thanks to their vision and their struggles, today there exists the Neot Kedumim institute, under whose auspices this book was written and published.

Like its predecessor, *Nature in Our Biblical Heritage*, this book too is intended as an aid to the reader visiting Neot Kedumim - The Biblical Landscape Reserve in Israel - while touring the site, as well as an additional study tool to be read at leisure. Furthermore, seeing the trees and shrubs mentioned in this book growing in Neot Kedumim can substantiate the material and greatly enrich the reader's comprehension and enjoyment.

Also like *Nature in Our Biblical Heritage*, this book does not deal with higher biblical criticism; **its main purpose is to show the vistas of the Land of Israel described in the Bible and Talmud as seen by Jewish tradition**. However, occasional reference is made to works by biblical scholars when deemed important to illustrate that without an intimate familiarity with the nature of the Land of Israel, students face insurmountable obstacles in understanding the written Word.

My work of the last decades developed from studies with my parents and as an outgrowth of work and joint research with them. It is, therefore, impossible to clearly identify what I learned from them, what developed from our collective research, and what materialized in the years following their death. For this reason I frequently use the plural "we," or "in our opinion," or "it seems to us." This wording is appropriate, too, because of the deep involvement of **Helen Frenkley** in all stages of the book's compilation, and the responsibility she undertook in writing the English version. The "we" is also called for because of the growing involvement of the entire Neot Kedumim staff in the joint creative effort. This book is part of the resultant fruit.

The contributions made by members of Neot Kedumim's staff to the contents and style of this book are too numerous to detail. However, special thanks must be extended to **Ruth (Narkiss) Precker** and **Shlomit (Feig) Keidar** who devoted many long hours to the painstaking Hebrew voweling of biblical quotations and proofreading the final text. The maps in the Hebrew and English versions were done thanks to the meticulous work of **Benny Dolinsky**.

Many readers of *Nature in Our Biblical Heritage* criticized the absence of an index. Therefore, we have included here indices to both volumes. The Hebrew indices were prepared by Shlomit (Feig) Keidar.

The index to the English version of *Nature in Our Biblical Heritage* is the work of **Pam Colwell** who spent a year at Neot Kedumim in the framework of university studies. The index to the English version of *Tree and Shrub in Our Biblical Heritage* was completed with the help of **Naomi Lerner**, who was also extremely helpful in the final proofreading of the English text, together with **Karen Baker**, both new additions to the Neot Kedumim staff.

Special thanks are due to **Rabbi Naftali Bar-Ilan** of Rehovot, who was kind enough to read the Hebrew manuscript and direct my attention to a number of important points.

Ezri Uval of the Hebrew University in Jerusalem generously gave of his time to check for inconsistencies in the Hebrew voweling.

Editing of the English version of *Tree and Shrub in Our Biblical Heritage*, written by Helen Frenkley, was done with the help of old friends: **Lillian Steinfeld**, a well-known editor in the United States, contributed many weeks of work to polishing the manuscript and double-checking all the biblical sources; **Paul Steinfeld**, Jewish educator, forester in up-state New York, and secretary-treasurer of Neot Kedumim Ltd. in the U.S., made valuable editorial suggestions. **Natalie Frenkley**, research analyst and editor, and **Alex Frenkley**, past deputy director of the Russian language division of the Voice of America, managed the rush job of editing the second draft of the English manuscript in one week of non-stop work.

In order to ease the reader's way, the text has been arranged in two unequal columns. The wide column deals with subjects that are connected by associative chains and may be read as a single narration. The narrow column contains supplementary information that can be compared to the branches of the wide-columned "tree," but that are no less important than the information in the "parent tree."

The graphic design of this book, done by the author with the assistance of Helen Frenkley, is intended to parallel its "older brother," *Nature in Our Biblical Heritage*. However we would not have dared tackle this immense task if not for the knowledge imparted to us over the years by two of the best graphic artists in Israel: **Zvi Narkiss**, who prepared the traveling educational exhibits of Neot Kedumim in the early years of its existence, and **Ran Caspi**, who designed many of Neot Kedumim's publications in Hebrew and English in subsequent years. Special thanks to **Shaul Akri** of Otiot Dfuss for his many talents and endless patience.

Despite the help received from all the friends mentioned above, this book would not have seen the light of day in its present form if not for the constant support of **Drora Hareuveni**, who encouraged me during the many periods when most of the author's time had to be spent on other aspects of Neot Kedumim's development.

Yitzhak Navon, fifth president of Israel, was also vociferous in his insistence that I persevere in writing despite the numerous other demands on my time. For his help during extremely difficult junctures and his participation in the joys of Neot Kedumim's development, our heartfelt thanks.

Neot Kedumim, 1984   Nogah Hareuveni

Beginnings of the Museum of Biblical Botany
Hannah and Ephraim Hareuveni, seen here in their home in the Bukharin quarter of Jerusalem, founded this collection in the early 1920's and donated it to the Hebrew University in Jerusalem when it was opened on Mount Scopus in 1925.

Foreword

> "Rabbi Shimon says: If one is walking along the road reciting, and suddenly stops his recitation to say: 'How pleasing is this tree! How pleasing is this furrow!', the Bible implies it is as though he endangers his life."
>
> (Avot 3,7)

There are those who interpret these words to imply that the Sages [5] of Israel had no affinity for nature or landscapes - that their sole interest was in studying the "dry law." However a deeper perusal of Rabbi Shimon's [21] words reveals a totally different point of view.

The Mishna [1] was not codified into written form for many generations. The Oral Law was learned by constant repetitious recitation, each subject linked to the next in an associative chain. Therefore we can logically assume that Rabbi Shimon's warning was intended for whoever was walking along the road **while reciting** the Oral Law; one must not break the train of thought to exclaim on the beauty of nature and risk losing the thread of Mishnaic discourse. This warning was given **specifically because** the sight of trees and furrows aroused deep emotions that could start the Jew on a totally different train of thought, unrelated to the Mishna he was learning by heart while walking along country roads. This break in concentration could cause him to lose the difficult and sometimes obscure associative links that thread together a whole range of *halakhot* [2]. Rabbi Shimon's warning was given exactly **because fields and forests never became humdrum vistas in Jewish eyes,** even after many generations of farming life in Israel.

This book intends to show that a major reason for this continuing involvement with nature was the fact that the landscapes of Israel and its phenomena of nature have been deeply intertwined with the entire field of study of Jewish tradition throughout the generations. Because of this, these vistas could never become commonplace. On the contrary, they have always raised in the imagination a particular aspect of individual or national life, whether as metaphor, parable, or symbol, whether in the Pentateuch, in the words of the prophets, in the Oral Law, or in *aggada* [3].

Our hope is that this book will bring the modern reader walking along the road (or riding by in his car) to see in the furrow and the tree numerous pictures associated with the lives of the ancient Israelites in the Land of Israel as they are reflected in biblical verses, the discussions and arguments of the Sages, and the tales of the midrashim [4]. Even though totally absorbed in studies, albeit indoors, in his mind's eye our reader will see the forests and the fields mirrored in the writings and say in his heart, without breaking off study: "How pleasing is this verse! How pleasing is this midrash! For both as one are found today in the tree and the furrow as they were seen by our ancestors in ancient days!"

This book deals with some thirty kinds of different-sized trees, "from the cedar of Lebanon to the hyssop that grows out of the rock." (I Kings 5:13) About half of these are part of lengthy descriptions and discussions; others are called forth only as corroborating witnesses and are therefore mentioned briefly or only in photographs.

The author and the staff of Neot Kedumim wrestled long and hard with the problems of which trees to include in this volume and in which order to present them to the reader. Each choice had its advantages and disadvantages, and each suggested order raised new problems and new solutions.

Each tree candidate presented to us its eligibility and demanded its rightful place in the book because of its role in the landscape of Israel and its influence upon it: some in ancient days, some in the present, and some as promised in the world to come. Since decisions had to be made, we organized the selected trees in historical groves ranging from the Garden of Eden to the "end of days" and the Messiah's coming. Once each one was planted in its alloted grove, each tree yearned to grow into the many places in other generations familiar to him from ancestral tales. And so the trees intermingled and created a goodly forest that, as happens in nature, also includes thickets. We have tried to open a path in this thick forest through associative links, using the method of the Sages as they navigated through the ocean of the Talmud and the depths of the Bible.

"Teach them...recite them...write them."
What is the biblical passage hinted at here? The Mishna does not explain. We believe that the reference is to the words of Deuteronomy 11:19-21, one of the most consequential passages in the Bible, written on the doorposts of Jewish homes:
"Teach them (the words of the Bible) to your children, reciting them **when you stay at home and when you walk along the road,** when you lie down and when you rise. Write them on the doorposts of your house and on your gates, **so that you** and your children **may live long** in the land that the Lord swore to your fathers to give to them, as long as the heavens are above the earth."
Therefore **if you stop** "reciting them...when you walk along the road," and study of the Bible and the Oral Law is broken off, **then you will not "live long"** and it is as though you have endangered your very life.

A vegetable or a tree?
In Mishnaic usage, every plant that puts out leaves from its below-ground stock is a vegetable; every plant that puts out leaves from above-ground stock, such as the cedar and the hyssop, is considered a tree.

Tree of life

"The tree of life (was) in the garden, and the tree of the knowledge of good and evil."

(Genesis 2:9)

"Happy he who has found wisdom, and has acquired understanding...for it is the tree of life to all who grasp it, and those who hold fast to it are happy."

(Proverbs 3:13,18)

Man did not stretch forth his hand to pick the fruit of the Tree of Life, and so did not gain the knowledge of life everlasting. But man did taste of the fruit of the Tree of Knowledge and his eyes were opened to find wisdom and seek discernment. Yet even as knowledge grew, the tree itself continued to arouse wonder. How does the tree harness sunlight and nourish itself from the air? (see pp. 22,23) How does the tree "know" to shed its leaves as the season of insufficient water approaches? What makes the tree hasten to grow a new generation of leaves in anticipation of the season of plentiful nourishment? These and many other questions perplexed humankind from the first taste of the fruit of the Tree of Knowledge. But the key puzzling mystery was the secret of the tree's strength in contrast to man's. How can a tree sustain life for hundreds and indeed thousands of years?

"There is hope for a tree, if it be cut down that it will sprout again and its fresh shoots will not fail. Though its roots grow old in the earth, and the stump is dying in the ground, if it scents water it may break into bud and make new growth like a young plant. But a man dies, and he disappears; man perishes and, lo, where is he?"

(Job 14:7-10)

Human awe at the seemingly immortal "Tree of Life" seen all around

The stump of an arbutus awakens to new life.

in field and forest brought numerous tribes and nations to worship trees, attributing to them supernatural powers. Religious ceremonies involving "holy" trees also spread among the Israelites during the First Temple period. Wooden idols were carved in imitation of the surrounding idol-worshippers, although the Bible teaches that there is only One God, Creator of heaven and earth, the tree being but one of His creations. The prophets, each in his own generation and in his own manner, struggled to inculcate this message. Consider but one paragraph in which Isaiah sarcastically describes the rationale of deifying the tree:

> "The woodworker draws his line taut and marks out a figure with a stylus; he planes the wood and measures it with calipers, and he carves it to the shape of a man, comely as the human form, to dwell in a house. For his use he cuts down cedars... He sets aside trees of the forest; or plants firs and the rain makes them grow. It becomes fuel for his fire; part of it he takes to warm himself, part he kindles and bakes bread; and part he makes into a god and prostrates himself; he shapes it into an idol and bows down before it! One half of it he burns in the fire and on this he roasts meat, so that he may eat his roast and be satisfied; he also warms himself at it and says, 'Wonderful! I can feel the heat, I am growing warm and see the fire!' Then what is left of the wood he makes into a god - his own carving! He bows down to it, worships it, and prays to it, saying, 'Save me, for you are my god!'"

> (Isaiah 44:13-17)

This method of ridiculing the worship of wood and stone was used not only by the prophets of the First Temple era. The midrash tells us that the Patriarch Abraham in his youth in the Chaldean city of Ur used this same sardonic gibe to point out to the masses the foolishness of pagan worship. Moreover:

> "Because he saw that they (the idols) were false, he placed them into a great bonfire and sent them up in flames."
> (Midrash Hagadol Breshit, parashat Noah 28)

Many years later when Abraham reached the barren desert surrounding Beersheva in the Negev, after he had spent a lengthy period encamped in shady forested mountain areas, the Bible tells us:

> "And Abraham planted an *eshel* tree in Beersheva, and called there on the name of the Lord."
> (Genesis 21:33)

The midrashim thread together the days of Abraham's youth, when he strove to convince those around him that wooden idols were false gods, to his old age, when he seated his guests in the shade of a tree he

The **First Temple** was built by King Solomon, dedicated in 952 BCE, and destroyed by the Babylonian king Nebuchadnezzar some 365 years later in 586 BCE.

p. 19

Flowering tamarisk branches of different species.

pp. 20-21

Early morning in a tamarisk grove
Water droplets adhere to the hygroscopic salt particles exuded by the branches; they will evaporate as the sun heats the air.

had planted and taught them to call upon the name of the Lord God of whose bounty they had eaten.

"Said Reish Lakish [38]: Do not read this as he (Abraham) 'called on the name of the Lord,' rather that he caused others to call on the name of the Lord. This teaches us that the Patriarch Abraham caused the name of the Holy One, blessed be He, to be uttered by every passerby. How? After they (the travelers) had eaten and drunk, they rose to bless him. He (Abraham) said to them: Did you eat what belongs to me? You ate of that which belongs to the God of the Universe! Thank, praise, and bless Him Who spoke and the world came into being."

(Sota 10a-b)

Field experimentation in the Talmud
The possibility of a plant subsisting on air was recognized by the Sages, as can be learned from Rabbi Ze'eira [45] (Eruvin 28b), who believed that the k'shuta (Cuscuta monogyna Vahl., dodder in English), which lives as a parasite on various wild plants such as the seerim (Poterium spinosum) and the hizma (Prosopis farcta Macbride, mesquite in English) nourishes itself from the air. But the Gemara brings proof against this opinion based on field experimentation: "For we saw that when we cut down the hizma, the k'shuta died." This means that the k'shuta does not subsist on air but rather nourishes itself from the soil through the hizma that serves as its host.

p. 22

The parasitic dodder
Cuscuta monogyna Vahl. (k'shuta in Hebrew) covers a Poterium bush. Inset: Close-up of dodder flowers.

Under
the tamarisk tree

What is the *eshel* tree that Abraham planted and why did he select it over all other trees? In many places in the vicinity of Beersheva a certain tree stands out. From afar its thick crown looks like gray-green pillows. Its heavy shade attracts passersby, shepherds, and their flocks. One of its Arabic names is *athal*, very much like the Hebrew *eshel*; in Latin, *Tamarix sp.*; in English, tamarisk. Anyone sitting in the morning shade of the tamarisk feels its pleasant coolness. If the sojourner raises his eyes to the tree's branches, he will be surprised to discover shiny droplets of water on the thin branchlets. These droplets, most plentiful after a humid night, evaporate towards noon. A lick of the tamarisk's branches reveals its secret: tiny salt crystals are exuded by the tree onto the leaves. At night, as the moisture increases in the cooler air, the water vapor adheres to the hygroscopic salt particles and condenses into droplets. With morning, as the sun warms the air, the water evaporates and so cools the tamarisk's branches. It appears that the Patriarch Abraham did not simply plant any tree upon arriving in Beersheva for a lengthy sojourn. He chose the tree whose shade is cooler than that of other trees. Moreover, the *eshel* can withstand heat and long dry spells by sending its roots deep down to find underground water. Not surprisingly, the *eshel* remains to this day in the vicinity of Beersheva, its ancient biblical name preserved by both nations sprung from Abraham: the descendants of Ishmael and the descendants of Isaac.

It does not take great flights of fancy to assume that Abraham planted more than just one tamarisk. A tamarisk branch planted in damp soil, especially if that soil is sand or loess (as is the case in the region of Beersheva), will quickly send out roots and branches. If water is available during the first growing season, the roots will seek out the damp soil strata and the tamarisk will continue to flourish without additional irrigation. Thus we can imagine that where Abraham settled he planted not one tree, but rather several trees, perhaps even a grove. The modern reader who can imagine an entire grove from the one word "tamarisk" still cannot compete with the rich imagination of the creators of the midrashim. The tamarisk, for all its pleasant shade, is not a fruit-bearing tree. The midrashic commentators therefore wondered what refreshments Abraham had to offer his guests in its shade.

"Said Reish Lakish [38]: This teaches that he created an orchard and planted all sorts of choice fruit therein."

(Sota 10a)

"Rabbi Judah [25] says: *Eshel* (means) orchard. Ask what you will (of it): figs, grapes, and pomegranates."

(Bereshit Raba 54,6)

Rabbi Nehemiah [26] really lets his imagination go, saying that the sojourner received from Abraham whatever his appetite desired: "a loaf of bread, meat, wine and eggs." (Bereshit Raba 54,6)

The delightful shade of the tamarisk is responsible for its widespread planting in other parts of Israel. Today, tamarisks are frequently grown as shade trees, especially in parks and along the boulevards of Israel's coastal cities.

The Sages commonly used the expression "large tamarisks" as a nickname for the greatest of the *tannaim* [6] of the first generations, in whose shade the *amoraim* [31] saw themselves taking shelter. When an *amora* cited one of the early *tannaim*, it was said that he "suspended himself from the large tamarisks," i.e., cited the higher authority of the *tannaim*. (Beitza 27a, Babba Batra 31b, and other places.) This same metaphor led the *amoraim* to say: "The great and respected tamarisks (the leading scholars) of the Diaspora are themselves equal only to the young chicks (the least) among the scholars and Sages residing in the Land of Israel." (Jerusalem Talmud, Baba Metzia, 1, 8)

Punning in Hebrew
"Ask what you will" (*Sh'al ma tish'al* in Hebrew): a play on words of the root of the Hebrew name *eshel* arrived at by inverting the first two letters.

Tamarisks: trees or ropes?
There are those who translate this expression using the Aramaic word for rope, *ashla*, thus arriving at the translation that the *amora* "supported himself by the big ropes." To us it seems more reasonable (and pleasant) to compare the great *tannaim* to shade-giving tamarisks rather than to ropes!

The tamarisk: protector of the railroad
At the advice of Dr. Ephraim Hareuveni, who served as the botanical adviser to the British Mandate Government in Palestine after World War I, tamarisk cuttings were planted in the dunes that sometimes covered the railroad ties between Rafiah and El Arish in the Sinai Desert. The results were not long in coming: The tamarisks spread over the dunes and stopped them from causing further damage to the railroad. Although there are other plants well suited to holding down sand dunes, such as the rotem *(white broom) mentioned on p.31, only the tamarisk provides the all-important extra benefit of uniquely cool shade.*

Samuel: the tamarisk on the mountain

Rashi [60], in his commentary on the verse "and Saul was then in Gibeah, sitting under the tamarisk tree in Rama" (I Samuel 22:6), says: "Saul sat in Gibeah thanks to the great tamarisk in Rama who was praying for his (Saul's) success." Who was this "great tamarisk" praying for Saul's success? This is clarified by Radak [63], using an expression of the Sages: "What does Gibeah have to do with Rama? Saul sits as king in Gibeah because of **the great tamarisk in Rama, who is Samuel** who was praying for his (Saul's) success." [Rama was Samuel's hometown, and Gibeah, Saul's.] "The (tribunal) court of Samuel the Ramaite" is mentioned several times in the Talmud (e.g., Yebamot 77a and Baba Kama 61a). The Sages saw the name "Rama" in this passage as hinting at the prophet Samuel and his tribunal court because of whom Saul was enthroned in Gibeah for two-and-a-half years. (See Ta'anit 5b.) This is the reason for viewing "the tamarisk in Rama" as symbolizing not only the prophet Samuel, but his tribunal court as well: "Rabbi Azariah [54] in the name of Rabbi Judah bar Simeon [50]: Tamarisk - this is the Sanhedrin [7]." (Breshit Raba 54,6)

But what about the tamarisk tree itself? It is a tree native to the coastal regions and the Negev Desert, so what is it doing in Gibeah - or Rama - which are located in the mountains? The picture of Saul and his company ("with all his courtiers in attendance upon him" [I Samuel 22:6]) sitting in the shade of the tamarisk that grew outside its natural habitat reminds us of the prophetess Deborah who "used to sit under the date palm of Deborah, between Rama and Bethel in the hill country of Ephraim, and the Israelites would come to her for justice." (Judges 4:5) The date palm, as the tamarisk, is also foreign to the hilly regions. It would seem too that the anomalous presence of these trees in the vicinity made them instantly recognizable from a distance, so it was logical that they were selected by leaders such as Samuel, Saul, and Deborah as distinctive places from which to officiate.

In the land of Benjamin
Rama, the home of Samuel; Gibeah, Saul's birthplace

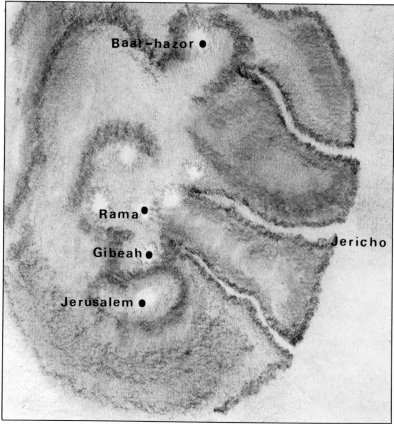

In the shade
of the white broom

There is a sudden transition between the cool shade under Abraham's tamarisks and the bright burning expanses of the Beersheva desert. Hagar felt this in full force when she was sent forth from Abraham's tents with Ishmael:

> "And she departed and wandered in the wilderness of Beersheva. When the water in the waterskin was finished, she thrust the child under one of the bushes."
>
> (Genesis 21:14-15)

Rabbi Meir [27] says that "one of the bushes" was the *rotem*, the white broom, "because *rotem* bushes usually grow in the desert." (Bereshit Raba 53,13 and other places.) As with the name *eshel*, so too the Hebrew name *rotem* is found intact in the Arabic word *rathem*. The Latin nomenclature, too, was taken from this name: *Retama raetam*.

Residents of Israel's coastal plain are familiar with the white broom as a medium-sized bush, growing primarily on sandy hills, as well as on gravel hills and red sandy loam. In the Beersheva desert and in the expanses of the Negev, the white broom grows in dry river beds to a height of two meters and more. Under optimum conditions it can even reach the size of a tree, with thick trunk and developed branches. It is wide on top and narrow at the bottom, giving welcome shade. Daytime breezes have easy access to the space under its branches, unlike other bushes growing in the habitat of the white broom (such as the *maluakh* and the *yitran;* see pp. 33, 54-56).

The *rotem* is easily recognizable by its grayish branches, which seem to be bare of leaves for most of the year. Towards the end of the rainy season the white broom wraps itself with young soft branches that bend easily in the breeze. This movement causes waves of silvery-gray light to pass through the bush, easily identifying it even from a distance. But the white broom is at its most beautiful during February-March, when it clothes itself in myriads of white papilionaceous flowers. Even the most reticent cannot help but exclaim over the gaiety that bursts forth in the wadis of the Negev as thousands upon thousands of tiny buds explode in white flower on the branches of the white broom. Delight and wonder increase as one approaches the flowering *rotem* to inhale the perfume the flowers exude, to observe the industrious bees carefully visiting each flower, and to peer closely at the deep purple calyxes and thin, brownish-purple lines encircling the white flowers.

Possibly Rabbi Meir's associative chain of thought that led him to identify "one of the bushes" under which Hagar placed Ishmael as the *rotem*, was also influenced by the place name Ritmah (Numbers 33:18-19), which is in the Wilderness of Paran where Ishmael dwelt after he was sent away with Hagar. (Genesis 21:21) The Wilderness of Paran is also the place from which the scouts were sent by Moses to explore the Promised Land. (Numbers 13:3) From this Rashi [60] compiled another midrash:

> "They sojourned in Ritmah because of the evil tongues of the scouts, as it is written: 'What will the slanderous tongue gain you (which is itself) a warrior's sharp arrows and *rotem* embers?' (Psalms 120:3-4)."

What is so special about *rotem* embers and what do they have in common with evil and slanderous tongues? The Jerusalem Talmud explains:

> "One may assume with regard to all other embers that once they are extinguished on the outside, the same is true on the inside. But *rotem* embers, though they are extinguished on the outside, still are not extinguished on the inside. In evidence, take the case of one who left burning *rotem* embers on *Sukkot* and returned on *Pesach* [a period of some five months comprising the rainy season in Israel] to find them still burning!" (Jerusalem Talmud, Pe'ah 1,1)

And the Babylonian Talmud states:

> "Said Rav Ashi: [59] Huna bar Natan [58] told me: Once we were walking in the wilderness and we had a leg of meat with us. We dressed the meat and cleaned it and placed it on some plants. While we were fetching wood, the leg regained its original skin texture and we roasted it. When we returned after twelve months, we saw those coals still glowing. When I came before Ameimar [57], he said to me: The plants were *samtari*. Those glowing coals were *rotem* (white broom) embers!" (Baba Batra 74b)

Ritmah in the Wilderness of Paran
The location of Ritmah in the Wilderness of Paran is verified by the conjunction of two verses in the book of Numbers. Chapter 33:18-19 lists Ritmah (as one of the stations of the Israelites during the Sinai wandering) coming right after Hazeroth. In chapter 12:16, the Wilderness of Paran comes after the encampment in Hazeroth.

p. 29

Folk medication
Samtari - *according to the Talmudic dictionary,* Arukh Hashalem, *the entry on* samtar: *"...or from the Syriac* samtaryn - *the juice of a weed used in bandaging (wounds), or that the name* samtar *consists of* sam *(drug) and the Persian word* tar *meaning wet, i.e., moist and effective medication."* The entry continues with the words of Dr. Avraham Kahut, editor of the Arukh Hashalem, *based on Pliny the Elder who raised the possibility that* samtaryn *in Syriac is the plant* Achillea *(yarrow). This is a small, extremely fragrant plant found in the Negev in the same growing regions as the* rotem; *it is used by the Bedouin as a cure for various illnesses.*

And in the Midrash Raba:

> "'Warrior's sharp arrows'- why select the arrow from all weapons? All other weapons strike close up, while this one (the arrow) strikes from afar. That is the way of evil tongues: What is said in Rome, kills in Syria. And not any ember, but only white broom embers - for all embers extinguish inside, while the broom embers, even when they are extinguished externally, still burn inside. So it is with someone who is the butt of slander; even though you have appeased him and he has (seemingly) been appeased, he still seethes on the inside. As it happened with a white broom bush that was lit and it burned eighteen months, winter and summer and winter." (Breshit Raba 95,l9)

Though it is clear that in all these midrashim there is more than a little exaggeration of the length of time the white broom embers retain their heat, it is a fact that these embers continue to burn beneath the ashes long after other embers have died out. Evidence of the recognition of this unique characteristic is also found in a rabbinic ruling relating to observance of Sabbath restrictions on cooking:

> "Rabbah bar bar Hana [47] said in Rabbi Johanan's [37] name: If he covered it (the fire) with ashes, yet it blazed up again, one may keep hot water upon it [if the water has already been heated to the desired temperature before the sabbath]; likewise a dish that has been cooked all it needs to be, even if upon white broom embers." (Shabbat 37b)

Rashi [60] explains here: "Broom embers are hotter than other embers and do not readily lose their heat."

The common use of *rotem* as kindling in cooking stoves led to the making of coals from the roots, trunk, and branches of the white broom. This trade was common among Negev Bedouin until very recent times, when it was forbidden by law in the modern State of Israel because of the threatened extinction of the white broom. Echoes of the existence of such an industry in ancient times come down to us through the words of Job bemoaning his bitter fate:

> "But now I am laughed to scorn by men of a younger generation, men whose fathers I would have disdained to put with the dogs who kept my flock...they who harvest the saltplant leaves and the root of the *rotem* is their bread." (Job 30:1,4)

Since, unlike the leaves of the saltplant, roots of the broom are totally inedible in any form, it is obvious that Job is speaking of white broom roots made into something that can be sold to **earn** one's bread. These young men who now scorn Job made embers from the roots of the white broom to sell in the marketplace. What lowlier livelihood can there be in the eyes of aristocratic Job than one that involves sitting by

Blazing embers on the Sabbath
The subject under discussion is the cooking fire, which was banked before the entry of the Sabbath (by covering the embers with ashes), but which blazed up again of its own accord.

The sand harness
The *rotem* is known as one of the most effective plants for holding back sand dunes. *Ratam* in Hebrew means to harness, rein in, hold in; hence, perhaps, its Hebrew name.

Truly leafless?
The *rotem* branches are not actually leafless, although they are so described in many botany textbooks. The *rotem* leaf is composed of two parts. The bottom part is like a concave scale, attached to the stem year round. From its axil it puts out a bud that can develop into a branch in the middle of the rainy season. The top part of the leaf, which is elongated and narrow, is present only on the young branches, which sprout in late winter. With the coming of the dry season, the upper part of the leaf falls off, leaving only the concave bottom scale.

Bread or warmth?
Some commentators have suggested a different voweling: לחמם *l'khamem* (to warm) instead of לַחְמָם *lakhmam* (their bread), i.e., "The roots of the *rotem* to *warm* them."

p. 30

Shady shelter in the desert
*The white broom (*Retama raetam*, rotem in Hebrew) in the desert around Beersheva.*

a fire night and day, black with soot and reeking of smoke? This description spills forth all Job's bitterness: He who in his time had been "like a king encamped with his troops" (Job 29:25) has now become in his impoverishment a target of scorn by nomads working at the lowliest trades.

Generations after Hagar, the prophet Elijah reached the Beersheva desert, fleeing from the wrath of Jezebel after he had killed the priests of Baal:

> "He was afraid and fled for his life. When he reached Beersheva ..., he left his servant there and himself went a day's journey into the wilderness. He came upon a white broom bush, and sat down under it and prayed for death: 'It is enough,' he said; 'now, Lord, take my life, for I am no better than my fathers before me.' He lay down under the white broom bush and, while he slept, an angel touched him and said, 'Rise and eat.' He looked, and there at his head was a cake baked on embers, and a pitcher of water. He ate and he drank and lay down again: The angel of the Lord came again and touched him a second time, saying, 'Rise and eat; the journey will be long for you.' He rose and ate and drank and, sustained by this food, he went on for forty days and forty nights to Horev, the mountain of God."
>
> (I Kings 19:3-8)

"The cake baked on embers" that Elijah ate under the white broom bush - what was it made of and who made it? The Bible does not explain. But one thing is certain: it was baked on embers. And on what coals would the cake have been baked if not white broom embers? These are the embers that retain fire and heat long after they appear to be dead ashes, and were blown into flame again from time to time in the Bible, in *halakha* and in *aggada*.

The traveler who looks on the ground beneath the white broom will also be able to see the mattress that served Elijah when he slept under the broom: a layer of thin, dry branches that drop off in the arid periods when the bush cannot supply nourishment to all the branches. These branches that cover the ground burn readily when gathered into a pile for kindling. Amazingly, this fire does not go out as quickly as expected. On the contrary, it grows quietly, producing great heat, dying down very gradually, leaving a pile of gray, charcoal-covered branches. A gentle puff into the pile proves that there is still a fire smoldering inside. The hiker who knows how to utilize this characteristic of the white broom branches will prepare a layer of broom embers on the ground to suit his size, cover them over with a layer of sand or fine soil to a depth of five to ten centimeters, and then enjoy a warm mattress in the cold desert night.

Saltplant leaves served on golden tables

The saltplant (*maluakh* in Hebrew), *Atriplex halimus* L., is one of the most important food plants in the Negev and other desert regions for both people and camels. Pass your cupped palm along the length of a saltplant branch from bottom to top, and you will come away with a handful of leaves. These leaves can be eaten raw. Usually they are too salty, however, and must be cooked.

"It once happened that King (Alexander) Yannai [Hasmonean king, 103-76 BCE] went to Kokhlit in the wilderness and conquered sixty towns there. On his return he rejoiced exceedingly and invited all the Sages of Israel. Said he to them, 'Our forefathers ate the saltplant when they were engaged in the building of the [Second] Temple; let us too eat the saltplant in memory of our forefathers.' So the saltplant was served on golden tables, and they ate." (Kiddushin 66a) This story reveals a legend, evidently widespread among the desert dwellers, about the saltplant eaten by the returning exiles from Babylon as a poor man's food when they were totally immersed in the rebuilding of the Holy Temple. Probably King Yannai heard this story during his march through the desert. Rashi [60] explains: The saltplant is a vegetable called *kakoli* in French, as in 'they who harvest the saltplant leaves' (Job 30:4). 'When they were totally immersed in the rebuilding of the Holy Temple': when they came from exile they were poor because they gave all their assets for the building of the Temple. Said Alexander Yannai, 'Now we too will eat the saltplant in memory of our forefathers' poverty in order to thank the Lord, Blessed be He, that He gave us success and riches.'"

Gathering saltleaves for cooking

33

The secret
of the burning bush

It is impossible to meander through the desert with Hagar and Ishmael, to sit under the *rotem* with Elijah, or to munch on the leaves of the saltplant with the youths who mocked Job and not inquire into the great wonder that Moses faced in the desert when he "was keeping the flock of Jethro, his father-in-law, the priest of Midian":

"And he led the flock deep into the wilderness and came to Horeb, the mountain of God. There the angel of the Lord appeared to him in the heart of the flame out of the *sneh*. Moses looked and, behold, the *sneh* burned with fire, and the *sneh* was not consumed. And Moses said, 'I must turn aside to see this wonderful sight, why the *sneh* is not burned.' When the Lord saw that Moses had turned aside to look, He called out to him out of the *sneh*, 'Moses, Moses.' And Moses answered, 'Here I am.' God said, 'Come no nearer; take off your shoes, for the place on which you stand is holy ground.'"

(Exodus 3:1-5)

What is this plant called *sneh* - so persistently translated simply as "bush" - which burned with fire but was not consumed? Some

p. 35

A branch of the "holy blackberry" (Rubus sanctus)
"As this sneh *that produces thorns and produces roses - so are the people of Israel..." (See p.40)*

p. 36

White broom at the peak of flowering

p. 37

White broom embers
Though the embers may seem extinguished on the outside, they still retain great heat and readily burst into flame with the lightest puff.

botanists and researchers raise the possibility that it was a fragrant bush that exudes a great quantity of essential oil. In such a case, they maintain, the volatile essential oil can catch fire around the bush but the flame will not touch the bush itself. Others are convinced that it is a semiparasitic plant that covers acacia trees, the *Loranthus acacia* Zucc., whose fire-red blossoms seemed to Moses like a flame that was not consuming the tree.

It must be suggested, however, that the search for a known desert phenomenon to explain the miracle of the "burning bush" is in itself based on a faulty assumption. If **we** find a plant that can explain what Moses saw, it is inconceivable that Moses, who was a shepherd in that very desert for so many years, was unfamiliar with it. What was it then that surprised him so? We should seek the possibility of an event that we have never experienced and that, as far as can be known, has never been experienced by any other person: an event that would be a one-time phenomenon even for Moses, who was most certainly witness to the most extraordinary incidents in the desert.

If we look at the details of the story, we find that the scene was revealed to Moses from a distance. When he decides to turn aside to see this amazing sight at close range, he hears the voice saying, "Come no nearer!" By emphasizing that Moses saw the burning *sneh* only from afar, perhaps the Bible points the way to a clearer understanding. In various regions of Sinai, as in other deserts and wilderness areas, mirages are well-known phenomena, caused by different density air layers refracting light waves. Images of lakes and trees which appear from a distance and disappear when approached are not the products of nomadic imagination. These are objects that do in fact exist in a distant place, and are transposed by the refracted light waves as images to the eye of the beholder who happens to be in the path of these light waves. It is therefore possible to imagine a situation in which the refracted light waves transmitted an image of a flame burning in some distant place and superimposed the image onto the *sneh* that Moses saw. "And behold, the *sneh* burned with fire, and the *sneh* was not consumed!" The singularly low probability of such a coincidence puts it in the category of a miracle. It is reasonable to believe that although Moses must surely have seen mirages, he had never seen anything as astounding as this and so exclaimed: "I must turn aside to see this wonderful sight, why the *sneh* is not burned."

Perhaps it is possible to find support for this explanation in the midrash: "'The heart of the flame' - was in the upper third of the *sneh* and upwards, just as the heart of man is in his upper third and upwards."

(Shmot Raba 2,5)

In other words, the author of this midrash believes that Moses saw the flame only in the upper third of the *sneh*. In fact, in many instances of a mirage, a light-reflecting layer of air forms tens of centimeters above ground, hiding from view all that is below it.

p. 38

Saltplant in the desert
The salt particles shimmer on the leaves of the maluakh (Atriplex halimus *L.*). *(See p.33)*

If this theory is accepted, it becomes unnecessary to search for a specific plant - bush, tree, or shrub - which is not consumed by fire. Therefore there is no reason not to accept the tradition passed on by the Sages that the *sneh* is a kind of blackberry bush. It is a dense, thorny bush growing near streams in many areas of Israel. This identification is also accepted by Christian tradition, from which comes the Latin name, *Rubus sanctus* Schreb., the "holy blackberry." The word *sneh* is very similar to the name of the "sharp-toothed rock" called "Seneh" described in the war that Saul and Jonathan waged near Michmas. (See I Samuel 14:4.) If we accept that the name *Sinai* is also related to the word *shen*, tooth, (*shinaim* - teeth), because of the sharp projecting shape of the granite rocks of the southern part of the peninsula [see Ephraim Hareuveni's article in *Sinai*, Mosad Harav Kook, vol.32], it is possible to relate the name *sneh* for the blackberry bush to its piercing, bent thorns that fasten into the flesh like sharp teeth. The *Rubus sanctus* grows into large thickets near sources of water and is thus an indicator for this precious commodity even from a considerable distance.

> "As this *sneh* growing on water - so are the people of Israel: they cannot grow except near the Torah, which is called water, as is said: 'Ho, all who are thirsty, come for water.'
>
> (Isaiah 55:1)

> "As this *sneh* that produces thorns and produces roses - so are the people of Israel, who include both righteous and wicked.

> "As this *sneh* that when a man puts his hand into it, he feels nothing [because the hooked thorns face downwards towards the center of the plant] and when he removes his

Modern taxonomy, too, assigns the *Rubus sanctus* (or *Rubus sanguineus* Friv.) to the **rose** family, *Rosaceae*.

***

Sinai - shinaim
The "toothed" mountains of southern Sinai

hand, he is scratched - so it was when the Children of Israel went down into Egypt, no one paid attention to them; when they left, they did so with signs and wonders and war.

"A pagan asked Rabbi Joshua ben Korha [20]: Why did the Lord God speak to Moses from the *sneh*? He answered him: And if He had spoken from the heart of a carob or a sycomore you would still have asked me the same thing! Obviously it will not be possible to let you go without a concrete answer. Why from the *sneh*? To teach you that there is not a single place where the Holy Spirit is not present, even in the *sneh*."

(Shmot Raba 2,5)

Thus from Abraham on we see the basic Jewish point of view that negates worship of "holy" trees despite awe before the tree's ability to withstand time and even injury. Although this wonder led to the creation of symbols and metaphors in Jewish folklore and literature, it did not develop into the pagan belief that the tree was inhabited by a deity or that it had godlike traits.

Sycomore not sycamore
The sycomore or Egyptian fig is the *Ficus sycomorus* L. dealt with at length on pp.83-92. It has nothing in common with the American plane tree *(Platanus occidentalis)* nor the English maple *(Acer pseudoplatanus)*, both of which are commonly called sycamore.

The sabbath breaker and the righteous man

One of the "trees" most impressive for its capacity to survive is undoubtedly the caper, *tzalaf* in Hebrew, *Capparis spinosa* (L.) in Latin.

> "Three are persevering: Israel among the nations,...the goat among cattle, and...the caper among the trees."

(Beitza 25b)

What is this unique perseverance that the Sages saw in the caper?

There are not many trees that persevere in so many different growing regions: in the hills and plains, in the valleys and along the coast, in rocky crags, in wilderness and desert areas, and even on stone house walls and fences. There are capers that grow in stone walls of houses and are repeatedly cut down year after year, yet continue to grow new branches that flourish and produce flowers and even fruit. Most impressive is the caper's ability to revitalize itself after fire. There is nothing comparable to the speed with which its below-ground stock can produce fresh green branches from the charred remnants. The caper has certainly earned its place among the persevering as the "persevering among trees," together with the Jewish people whose similar feats of survival make it the "persevering among nations."

As we shall see, this bush crops up in many generations of Jewish history: from the period of the wandering in the Sinai Desert, through the settlement of the Land of Israel by the twelve tribes, to the ocean of Talmudic legal rulings, from there to early and late midrashim, and on to the hopes of the world to come.

> "And while the children of Israel were in the wilderness, they found a man gathering kindling on the sabbath day. Those who had caught him in the act brought him to Moses and Aaron and all the community, and they kept him in custody, because it was not clear what was to be done with him. The Lord said to Moses, 'The man must be put to death; he must be stoned by all the community outside the camp.' So they took him outside the camp and all stoned him to death, as the Lord had commanded Moses."

(Numbers 15:32-36)

According to Rabbi Akiva [16], (Shabbat 96b) "the one who gathered kindling," whose name the Bible does not reveal, was none other than

p. 43

The sharp caper = Tzalaf khad
In winter the dry caper branches serve as excellent kindling.
Inset: *A lone caper west of the Bitter Lake in Egypt*

p. 44

"The persevering among the trees"
right
A young caper branch bursts forth from an exposed, "dead" root.
left
The caper thrives even in arid wilderness.

42

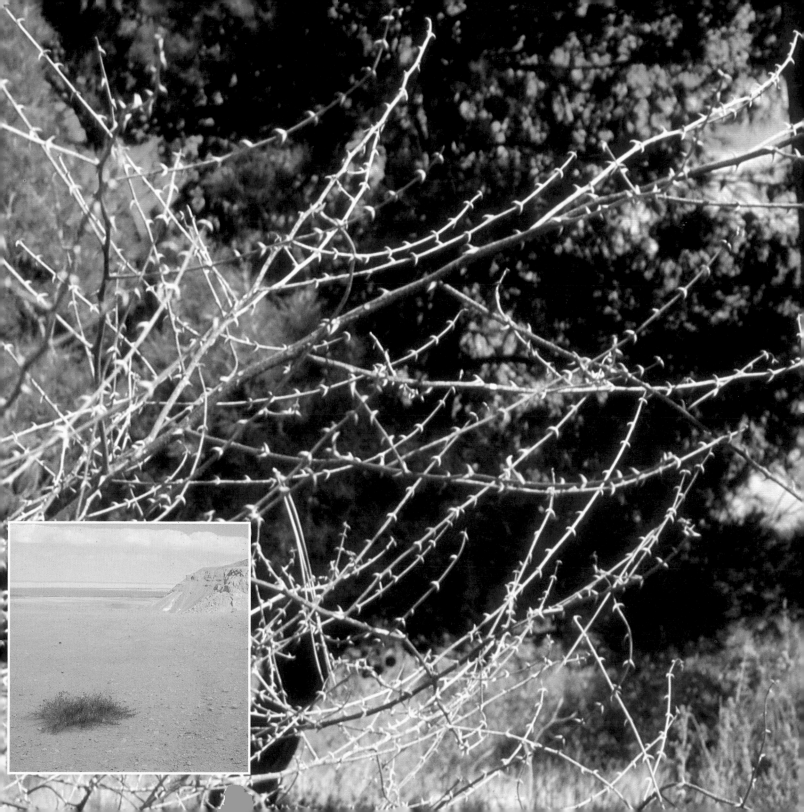

Tzlofkhad (Zelophehad) who "died in the wilderness...for his own sin" as attested to by his five daughters. (See Numbers 27:3.) He is the same Tzlofkhad of whom it is said: "The caper tree is hinted at in his name: *tzalaf* (caper) + *khad* (sharp) = the sharp caper." (See p.48 for full midrash.)

We believe that familiarity with the caper will enable the reader to unravel the chain of associations that brought Rabbi Akiva to say "the one who gathered kindling is Tzlofkhad."

The caper tree stands leafless during the rainy season. The thin branches die and dry out, providing perfect kindling in a season when there is little else to burn in Israel. Rabbi Akiva, who was a shepherd in his youth, must have also used the caper in rainy weather. Rabbi Akiva linked two separate biblical chapters (Numbers 15 and 27), relating two separate events, and concluded that the nameless kindling gatherer who died for the sin of breaking the sabbath was in fact Tzlofkhad, "who died for his sin in the wilderness" (Numbers 27:3), but whose specific sin is not mentioned. The dry caper was a logical plant for the gatherer of kindling to have collected.

But the caper's main claim to fame is not as kindling in winter but in the crops it produces in summer.

> "Rabbi Eliezer [13] says: The caper shall be tithed on its *timorot* (the young leaves at the tip of the branches), its *avionot* (the fruit), and its *cafrisin* (the young flower buds). Rabbi Akiva says: Only the *avionot* shall be tithed because only they are fruit."
>
> (Ma'asrot 4,6)

The caper "fruit" we find today in small jars on supermarket shelves are actually the *cafrisin* - the unopened caper flower bud. It is not fruit at all in the botanical sense, although it is a crop harvested from the caper bush for food. This accounts for the debate between Rabbi Eliezer and Rabbi Akiva. In Israel it is possible to see also the marinated fruit of the caper (that develop from the pistil after the flower has been pollinated), called *avionot* in Talmudic times. A condiment was also made from the *timorot*, the tenderest young leaves at the tips of the branches.

The caper is a native of Israel and can be found growing wild almost everywhere in the country. But only those in the know will bother to harvest the unopened buds or the fruit from all these capers and marinate them into tasty homemade condiments. Not so in Talmudic times. From the discussions of the Sages in the Mishna [1], Tosefta [1], and Gemara [1], we learn that the caper was cultivated as a full-fledged agricultural crop:

> "The caper - the School of Shammai [8] says it is *kilayim* [forbidden to grow] (in a vineyard) and the School of Hillel [8] says it is not *kilayim*. Both agree that the caper is subject to *orla* [the prohibition against making use of a tree's fruit for the first three years]." (Tosefta Kilayim 3,17)

Why reveal what the Bible has hidden?

The Gemara relates that Rabbi Judah ben Bathyra [17] was uncomfortable with the identification of Tzlofkhad as the kindling gatherer. He said, "Akiva, you will have to render judgment in either case: If you are right (that Tzlofkhad is the kindling gatherer), the Bible has hidden this, yet you reveal it! And if not (if the kindling gatherer is not Tzlofkhad) then you have slandered a righteous man (Tzlofkhad)!" (Shabbat 96b)

Another caper name

There is another biblical reference to a man with the name *tzalaf* - caper - "Hanun, the sixth son of Tzalaf" (Nehemia 3:30) among the returning Babylonian exiles who rebuilt the walls of Jerusalem.

Taxation problems and name inversions

Talmudic usage gave an additional name to the caper, *nitzpa*. (Brakhot 36a and 40b) The *nitzpa* is counted among the *kalin sh'b'dmai*. (Dmai 1,1) In the days of the Temple, a tenth part - a tithe - of each type of cultivated produce was paid as a tax to the Temple. It was the responsibility of every Israelite **buyer** to make certain that the **owner** of produce had already set aside the applicable tithe. However, several crops that grew wild could also be cultivated and raised for profit. These crops were referred to as *kalin sh'b'dmai*, meaning that it was not obligatory to make certain that the tithes on them had been paid, since there was no foolproof way of checking whether the fruit came from wild or domesticated trees or shrubs. Since the caper was tithed like all agricultural produce, it is reasonable to assume that the name *nitzpa* refers to the **wild** caper and not to the cultivated caper which is the *tzalaf*.

Perhaps this name developed from a letter inversion of the word *napatz*, meaning to crack or split. What better than the caper can split open rocks and crack walls, fences, and stones when it breaks through into wild growth? As to the name *tzalaf*, perhaps it too comes from a letter reversal of the verb *patzal*, also meaning to split or crack. When the fruit ripens, it splits open along the length of the fruit, thereby exposing the black seeds to birds who eat and thus disperse them. The name of the caper and letter reversals cannot be complete without mentioning the Arabic name of the *tzalaf* - *latzaf*, which, of course, is a variant inversion of the Hebrew name.

This name, *latzaf*, misled the famed 19th century British explorer of the land of Israel, Henry Tristram, and in his footsteps several other scholars, to identify the *tzalaf* (caper) as the *ezov* (hyssop). His supposition was that the Arabic word *latzaf* (which is pronounced *lasaf*) is made up of *el-asaf*, **the** *ezov* (hyssop).

Paraphrasing Rav Judah [36] speaking in the name of Rav [35]: Concerning capers grown in an area where it is uncertain whether the prohibition against "forbidden fruit" -orla- has been observed, discard the fruit and eat the buds. (from Brakhot 36a)

From this we learn that the caper was a cultivated crop, planted for its various food uses, else why the concern with the "forbidden fruit"? In fact this was clearly stated:

> "The caper is planted for the purpose of its flower bud... However Rav Nahman ben Isaac [53] says: The caper is planted for the purpose of its leaves (the *timorot*)."
>
> (Brakhot 36a)

Whether the desired crop was the flower bud, the leaf tip, or the fruit there is no question that the Israelites planted the caper as an income producer which bears three different types of crops.

> "Rabban Gamaliel [12] sat and expounded: In the world to come trees will give fruit every day, as it is said: 'It will put out branches and bear its fruit.' (Ezekiel 17:23) Not only shall it put out a new branch every day, but fruit as well! One of his students scoffed at him, saying: But it is written, 'There is nothing new under the sun.' (Ecclesiastes 1:9) (Rabban Gamaliel) replied: 'Come and I will show you an example

From *cafrisin* to caper
The name *cafrisin* given by the Sages to the flower bud is the root of the English name of the plant, caper, as well as the Latin name, *Capparis spinosa*.

The fruit and the foreskin
"When you enter the land and plant any tree for food, you shall regard its fruit as forbidden. Three years it shall be forbidden to you, not to be eaten. In the fourth year all its fruit shall be set aside for jubilation before the Lord; and only in the fifth year may you use its fruit." (Leviticus 1:23-25)

It is thus clear that the injunction concerning forbidden fruit holds true only for planted and cultivated fruit trees. Obeying this commandment ensures the development of the root system and the healthy growth of the young sapling's trunk and branches, especially if the grower takes care to remove the flowers before they begin to produce embryonic fruit.

The literal translation of this verse would render "forbidden fruit" as "uncircumcised fruit." The Hebrew word used is *arelim*, meaning uncircumcised. In this context the flower is a kind of "foreskin" - a covering or wrapping of the embryonic fruit hidden within the flower.

in this world.' He went out (with the students) and showed them a caper."

(Shabbat 30b)

To what special characteristic was Rabban Gamaliel alluding when he specified the caper as an example in this world of a tree that gives fruit every day, as all fruit trees shall when the Messiah comes? The answer is apparent to anyone who has worked for high quality yields in harvesting capers.

During its lengthy flowering season, the caper produces new flowers every day. Each flower remains open for fewer than twenty-four hours. Towards evening the bud opens into a flower; in late morning of the following day as the heat increases, the flower wilts, leaving the embryonic fruit to protrude on top of the pistil. The caper actually does give new fruit each day of its extraordinarily long flowering season!

As was noted, in the opinion of Rabbi Eliezer [13], the flower buds of the caper bush are also considered a fruit subject to the tithe. The same is true for the *timorot*, the leafy tips of the young branches that develop on the caper during its seven-month growing period. To get a prime yield, the harvesters must go out to the caper bush every day throughout these seven months, because otherwise the yield of a missed day will be lost. The flower buds (capers), the *timorot*, and the

The caper and Neot Kedumim
When it came to the selection of the emblem for Neot Kedumim - The Biblical Landscape Reserve in Israel - we wanted a symbol of both the history of the educational institution and of its aspirations for the future. We also searched for an emblem that would represent the principal concepts of Neot Kedumim. The caper was selected from among many other candidates because of its numerous symbolic virtues. The caper's roots in the literary sources of Judaism spread across generations of history: from the days of the wandering in the Sinai Desert, to the homilies, stories, and other literature of the sixteenth century Kabbalists. The caper is useful to the shepherd and the farmer, and it appears on the table of peasant and king. And what plant is better suited to inspire the Neot Kedumim team to produce fruit in its daily work!

Even its perseverance, expressed in the caper's renewed growth after each setback, and its ability to take root in barren, dry rock and draw forth moisture and nourishment - all these only hint at what Neot Kedumim has experienced from the time such an institution was first envisioned by Ephraim and Hannah Hareuveni in the early years of the twentieth century and until its creation and flowering in the last decade.

The lovely caper flower was converted into a stylized design by the well known Israeli graphic artist, Zvi Narkiss.

The caper flower
From closed bud to open flower in less than two hours.

fruit *(avionot)* not picked one day and left for the next will no longer be at their best; because of the rapid growth of the caper bush, they will be too large and bitter. The opposite also holds true: The yield must not be picked too early, not by a single day, else there will not yet be that unusual taste so prized in the caper. This necessity of harvesting the caper every day is what gave rise to the impression that it gives fruit every day.

But Rabban Gamaliel did not content himself with a mere reminder of the caper. He took his students and **showed** them the caper bush. It would seem that he taught them to look at one branch of the caper, from the tip down to the base, seeing in progression the young caper buds, flower buds waiting to blossom, one (sometimes two) open flowers, one (or two) wilted flowers with the embryonic fruit peeping out from among the drooping petals, and a row of fruit: the youngest closest to the wilted flower and the oldest nearest the base of the branch. In short, an example in this world of a tree in the world to come!

> "This is a story of a righteous man who found a break in his fence and was about to go out to repair it when he remembered that it was the sabbath. And the righteous man refrained from fixing the break. A miracle occurred: A caper bush grew (closing off the break in the fence), and he and his family lived off (the income) from that caper for the rest of their lives."
>
> (Shabbat 150b and in different versions in other sources)

One other important aspect of the caper is its extreme thorniness. Each leaf has two companion thorns shaped like hooks bent inward towards the center of the plant. There is no problem in thrusting a hand downward into the center of the caper; no pain is felt until one tries to withdraw one's hand. Then these barbed hooks jam into flesh and cloth! The caper is not a plant to approach carelessly, for it has ample protection against the unwary. The caper that grew in the gap in the righteous man's fence was well suited to mend the fence and keep out unwanted intruders.

The soul of the sabbath-breaker, Tzlofkhad, who gathered kindling, had transmigrated to this righteous man who refrained from breaking the sabbath. The original Tzlofkhad died for his sin of breaking the sabbath, but the righteous man was able to earn his living from the selfsame caper (paraphrased from *Dvash L'pi*, Hida). Hida continues: "The caper tree has its meaning hidden in its name: *tzalaf* (caper) + *khad* (sharp) = the sharp caper."

Despite the sharp criticism expressed by Rabbi Judah ben Bathyra [17], Rabbi Akiva's opinion prevailed in midrashic literature. In Kabbalistic [64] tradition, Tzlofkhad is also identified with the kindling gatherer whose soul did not rest until it came into the body of that (also nameless) righteous man who "refrained from wickedness and kept

Neot Kedumim's fencing
In Neot Kedumim - The Biblical Landscape Reserve in Israel, caper bushes have been planted as part of the fencing of the garden network periphery - a most effective hedge!

Hida - Hayyim Joseph David Azulai (1724-1806) was born in Jerusalem and traveled widely. Hida was regarded by the Jewry of the Ottoman Empire and of Italy as the leading scholar of his generation. He was a student of Kabbala, bibliographer, author, and one of the first collectors of Jewish folk stories in a systematic manner. He deals with the matter of Tzlofkhad as taken from *Yalkut Reuveni*, a compilation of homilies from the seventeenth century. The subject also appears in different versions in other sources.

p. 49

Yitran ropes to draw water from the cistern
bottom center
A young yitran *bush (Thymelea hirsuta) in the desert*
left
Flowering yitran
top
Soldiers inspect the long rope they made from yitran
bottom right
The rope is used to draw refreshing water from the desert cistern
(see pp. 54-56)

pp. 50-51

At sunset
Each evening a new flower blossoms on the caper branch.

the sabbath." What reward could be more appropriate than that the caper provided the livelihood for the righteous man and all his house!

In fact, it turns out that the caper provided the livelihood for the family of the first Tzlofkhad as well:

"A claim was presented by the daughters of Tzlofkhad... Their names were Mahlah, Noah, Hoglah, Milcah, and Tirzah. They appeared at the entrance of the Tent of the Presence before Moses, Eleazar the priest, the chieftans, and all the community and spoke as follows: 'Our father died in the wilderness. He was not among the company of Korakh that plotted together against the Lord; he died for his own sin and left no sons. Is it right that, because he had no son, our father's name should disappear from his family? Give us our property on the same footing as our father's brothers.' So Moses brought their case before the Lord, and the Lord spoke to Moses and said: 'The claim of the daughers of Tzlofkhad is right. You must allow them to inherit on the same footing as their father's brothers. Let their father's patrimony pass to them.'" (Numbers 27:1-7)

The daughters of Tzlofkhad won their claim to their rightful inheritance in the Land of Israel. Indeed their case set a precedent in biblical law: "When a man dies leaving no son, his patrimony shall pass to his daughter." (Numbers 27:8) Where was their patrimony in Israel? Archeological data reveal place names all concentrated in the northern regions of the mountains of Ephraim in Samaria identical with the names of three of the daughters of Tzlofkhad (Noah, Hoglah and Tirzah). Many slopes in this area are composed of poor limestone on which even the sturdiest of fruit trees cannot produce good crops. The caper, on the other hand, grows extremely well in this soil and to this day can be seen there as a wild plant. It is logical to assume that the Israelites utilized such areas to cultivate capers. The Kabbalistic midrash which ties the caper to Tzlofkhad and to the righteous man and his livelihood seems, therefore, to have roots in the reality of the ancient settlement of Israel.

p. 52

Rabban Gamaliel's methodology

upper left
"(Rabban Gamaliel) went out and showed them a caper."

bottom left
Jug-shaped bulb of the white squill

right
"(Rabban Gamaliel) dreamt he saw white hatzavim filled with soot."

White squill and the unworthy students
It is told of Rabban Gamaliel of Yavne [12] that he decreed: "No student who is not honest in thought as in deed shall enter the Academy!" (Brakhot 28a) For many years after the destruction of the Second Temple, Rabban Gamaliel served as *nasi* (head) of the Sanhedrin [7] in Yavne and worked for the unification of the people around one spiritual center and the determination of one code of legal rulings *(halakha)* for all Israel. In striving to achieve this goal, he relentlessly wielded his authority over the Sages who differed from the majority opinion. When the Sages of the Academy could no longer bear his strictness, they dismissed him from his post and instead appointed Rabbi Eleazar ben Azariah [15] as head of the Academy. "On the day he (Rabban Gamaliel) was discharged, the doors were opened and permission was given to all students to enter" [without checking to see whether they were "honest in thought as in deed"]. On that day hundreds of benches had to be added in the Academy. "Rabban Gamaliel's conviction was shaken" when he saw so many new students coming to learn after his removal from office. "He said: Perhaps, Heaven forbid, I hindered study from Israel? He dreamt he saw white *hatzavim* filled with soot." (Brakhot 28a) This dream reassured him that he had been right after all.

Commentators interpreted this dream to mean that Rabban Gamaliel saw white jugs. In this view, the white jugs filled with soot represented those students whom Rabban Gamaliel prevented from entering the Academy because their thoughts were not as honest as their deeds. But why would this **reassure** Rabban Gamaliel?

Another interpretation of the dream was given by Ephraim and Hannah Hareuveni (in their book, *The White Squill and the Asphodel*, Jerusalem, 1941). They based their interpretation on the fact that the Hebrew word *hatzav* has two different meanings: clay jug as well as the plant *Urginea maritima* (L.) Bak. - white squill. The white flowers of the squill appear all over Israel at the end of summer, many weeks before the appearance of their broad leaves in the beginning of the rainy season. However, it is sometimes possible to see the flower-bud-covered stalks of the white squill around Hannuka, in December, when the leaves are already large and fully grown. Close inspection reveals that these stalks bear only flower buds (with only extremely rare instances of one or two open flowers). These buds are white just as are those of the normal white squill, but a bit more swollen. When opened, these buds turn out to be filled with a kind of black "soot" - a fungus that has entirely destroyed the inside of the bud.

If we accept the explanation that these are the *hatzavim* that are "white on the outside but black on the inside" that Rabban Gamaliel saw in his dream, it is easy to understand why this dream reassured him that his strict criteria did not after all "hinder study" - these diseased buds will never develop into flowers nor will they produce seeds. So with the students whose thoughts are not as their deeds, who were allowed to enter the Academy after his departure - they will never contribute anything of value to the study of the Torah.

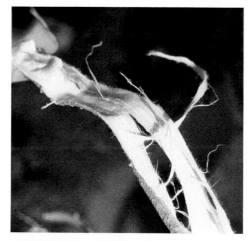

Samson's rope

With the settlement of the tribes of Israel in the Promised Land, judges arose from time to time to lead the people in battle and to adjudicate between the tribes. The most unusual among the judges was Samson; he specialized in one-man operations against the Philistines, who occasionally invaded the areas settled by the Israelites. Samson's daring exploits publicized his name throughout the Philistine settlements and enabled him to protect his people's borders most effectively by creating constant deterrents.

The story of one of Samson's actions was brought to light by Dr. Ephraim Hareuveni [*Hayetarim halakhim asher lo khoravu,* "Leshoneinu," v.12, booklet 1-2, 1942] after he had studied one of the interesting plants growing both in the many dry river beds of the Negev (together with the white broom and the saltplant), as well as on the coarse sandhills and sandy loam of the coastal plain - areas that were in Philistine hands in Samson's time.

In Arabic the plant is called *mitnan,* a word taken from *tamtin* or *tamtan* meaning the guyrope of a tent - *yeter* in Hebrew. This plant's Hebrew name, suggested by Dr. Ephraim Hareuveni, is *yitran,* derived from *yeter*. This was the name of Yitran ben Dishon of the descendants of Esau (Genesis 36:26 and I Chronicles 1:41) and of Yitran ben Tzofakh (I Chronicles 7:37). The *yitran* is, in fact, the best plant for making ropes. The Latin name is *Thymelea hirsuta* (L.) Endl.

The leaves of the *yitran* are small and flush with the branch. They have a thick membrane on the bottom (outside) and on the upper side (inside) they are covered with white, feltlike hairs. These characteristics are related to the arid regions in which the *yitran* grows. Its roots penetrate to the deep strata of the soil, enabling the plant to remain fresh and green throughout the year in Israel, even in desert areas.

The *yitran*'s branches are bent, especially at the tips. This gives the bush a soft shape, most prominently in the bow-shaped young branches that whip about rapidly in the breeze. This characteristic makes it easy to distinguish the *yitran* even at a distance from similarly colored and shaped plants growing in its habitat. The *yitran* also has a sharp sulfurous odor that is diffused when the branches are rubbed or when the bark is peeled to make ropes.

Familiarity with the *yitran* plant and the lengthy, complex rope-making process enables us to understand how Samson outmaneuvered the Philistines and at the same time publicized his strength far and wide.

> "Samson fell in love with a woman named Delilah who lived in the Wadi (valley of) Sorek. The lords of the Philistines went up-country to see her and said, 'Coax him and find out what gives him his great strength, and how we can master him, bind him, and so torture him; then we will each give you eleven hundred pieces of silver.' So Delilah said to Samson, 'Tell me what gives you your great strength, and how you can be bound and tortured?' Samson replied, 'If they bind me with seven *yetarim* that are moist and have never dried, then I shall become as weak as a normal man.' So the lords of the Philistines brought up to her seven *yetarim* not yet dry, and she bound him with them. She had men already hidden in her room. Then she called out to him, 'Samson, the Philistines are upon you!' Whereupon he snapped the *yetarim* as a strand of tow comes apart at the touch of fire. So the secret of his strength remained unknown." (Judges 16:4-9)

In the foothills of the Judean mountains where Samson lived in "Mahaneh Dan between Zorah and Eshtaol" (Judges 13:25), the *yitran* does not grow. Ropes made from *yitran* fibers could certainly have been bought in the local marketplace, but Samson's instructions to Delilah explicitly prevented this, for he told her that they must be "moist and never been dried." In other words, he ensured that these would be **freshly picked** and not rewetted, thus precluding their

Making ropes from yitran

The bark is cut at the bottom of the branch to a depth at which the woody part of the branch is felt. The bark is then peeled upwards, making certain that only one strip is taken from each branch in order to avoid girdling (and thus killing) any single branch. The bark slips off easily as a thin strip, long and strong, together with all the small branchlets growing out from it. The strips of bark must then be carefully cleaned by hand or with a knife until they are smooth and easy to work. A few strips are held together and folded in half, and then twisted together between the palms of both hands. When the thickness of the rope begins to diminish, new fibers are added, also folded in half, so that a rope of unlimited length can be made without a single knot or weak point. Making ropes from yitran *fibers takes time and patience, but the result is a rope strong enough even to tow a jeep from hubcap-deep mud. The* yitran *strips should not be held between the teeth, because the sap causes an extremely unpleasant and long-lasting irritation in the throat.*

purchase in the local marketplace as ready-made, dry ropes that Delilah could have wetted before using. Samson's conditions required the Philistines to get an enormous amount of work done in one day: they had to gather huge quantities of *yitran* fibers on the coastal plain where they grow; these had to be worked clear of twigs in preparation for the actual plaiting; immediate plaiting - before the strands dried out - all the while paying strictest attention to the quality of the rope that had to be plaited with special care to ensure the greatest possible strength. All this required marshalling a number of experienced teams capable of finishing the work in the morning hours. For after the ropes were finished, they still had a long journey of at least twenty kilometers from the land of the Philistines to Samson's home - many hours walk in the heat of the day. All this activity must have caused great curiosity in the Philistine villages along the way. Quite a crowd must have gathered to see the capture and submission of the fabled Samson.

One can almost hear the cries of amazement and excitement from the crowds at Samson's unbelievable feat when he snapped seven ropes made from this incredibly strong *yitran* fiber as easily as "a strand of tow comes apart at the touch of fire." It takes but little to imagine how the story of Samson's feat grew like wildfire in the telling and retelling as the people returned to their villages and embroidered upon what they had seen and heard. Samson succeeded in multiplying the deterrent power of his actual strength by applying an intuitive understanding of crowd psychology in this clever "public relations" ploy.

Desert flypaper
Another use of the *yitran*, as shown by tent dwellers in the Negev, is as flypaper! A *yitran* bush is wetted with sugar water and tied to the central tent pole. Flies settle on the *yitran* in vast numbers and seem to stick to the leaves. In the evening the fly-studded shrub is carefully removed and thrown into a nearby gully.

p. 57

The atad's *roots are widespread, leaching all the nutrition from the soil surrounding the tree.*
upper left
The crab apple-like fruit of the atad.

"Come
and take refuge
in my shade"

Gideon was another judge in Israel; his activities centered in the north of the country. With the help of a handful of select fighters and the use of psychological warfare, he succeeded in routing the Midianite hordes who had invaded the eastern lands of Israel. (See Judges 7-8.) After the great victory, Gideon was asked by the people to continue to lead them and even to found a dynasty: "Rule over us - you, your son and your grandson as well, for you have saved us from the Midianites." (Judges 8:22) Gideon refused, choosing to return to his home and farm.

But after Gideon's death, one of his sons decided that the kingship was not a bad idea. He took the name "Avi-melekh" (Abimelech), meaning "my father is king" (Judges 8:31), and talked his relatives in Shechem into supporting his bid for monarchy. His first step was to get rid of those who could oppose him, namely the seventy sons Gideon had had by his wives in the town of Ofrah. This he did by killing them all "on one stone." (Judges 9:5) Afterwards Avimelekh returned to his mother's hometown of Shechem as a hero, covered with fame and glory. "Then all the citizens of Shechem and all Beth-millo came together and made Avimelekh king beside the oak pillar that was in Shechem." (Judges 9:6) But Jotham, the only one of Gideon's sons to hide and escape the slaughter, could not acquiesce without a murmur to the installation of Avimelekh as king. While the crowd was celebrating the coronation,

p. 58

"Come and take refuge in my shade."

top
The atad (Ziziphus spina-christi) *gives shade even when leafless.*
bottom
The yikshat (Lycium) *casts no shade even when in full leaf.*

59

"Jotham went and stood on the summit of Mount Gerizim. He cried at the top of his voice: Listen to me, you citizens of Shechem, and may God listen to you:

"Once upon a time the trees came to anoint a king, and they said to the olive tree: Be king over us. But the olive tree answered: What, leave my rich oil by which God and man are honored, to come and rule over the trees?

"So the trees said to the fig tree: Then will you come and be king over us? But the fig tree answered: What, leave my good fruit and all its sweetness, to come and rule over the trees?

"So the trees said to the grapevine: Then will you come and be king over us? But the grapevine answered: What, leave my wine that gladdens God and man, to come and rule over the trees?

"Then all the trees said to the *atad*: Will you then be king over us? And the *atad* said to the trees: If you really mean to anoint me as your king, then come and take refuge in my shade; if not, fire shall come out of the *atad* and consume the cedars of Lebanon."

(Judges 9:7-15)

It is impossible to fully comprehend the words of Jotham in this "parable of the trees" without knowing the true identification of the *atad*, to which Avimelekh is compared.

"'Then all the trees said to the *atad*' - this is Avimelekh. Just as the *atad* is covered with thorns, so Avimelekh was covered with evil deeds."

(Midrash Tanhuma Vayere 29)

This hint by Rabbi Tanhuma bar Abba [56] still does not reveal the central character in the parable of Jotham.

Many translators rendered the *atad* as bramble, a small, thorny bush. In fact, most commentators have identified the *atad* with the bush of the genus *Lycium*, the best known of which is the *Lycium europaeum* L. This is a tangled bush with thorny branches bent like bows. Even from afar, these bow-shaped branches are its distinguishing feature. For this reason, Dr. Ephraim Hareuveni called the bush *Lycium* by the name *yikshat* (from the Hebrew word for bow, *keshet*), a name that quickly spread among Israel's nature lovers. Another characteristic that distinguishes this plant from afar is its relative stillness in the wind. Even in a strong breeze, when most bushes and trees bend and sway, there is no perceptible movement in the *yikshat*. This "bramble" grows from half a meter to over two meters in height; some especially large specimens can reach three meters. Its diameter can also reach two meters and more. Since it commonly grows with others of its species, it creates tangled thickets. For this reason, Arab farmers grow it as an effective fence. Another characteristic of the *yikshat* is that the trunk is not readily visible. Whether because the lower branches sweep the ground with their "bows" or because of its growth pattern, many branches seem to grow up from the ground without a single central trunk. Because of this, the *yikshat* has no shade, except for the lengthy shadows cast by any object in early morning or late afternoon.

In midsummer the *Lycium europaeum* - the *yikshat* - begins to shed its leaves. By the time the cold rainy days arrive, the boughs of the bush reveal their grayish-white bark. For long months the bush looks dry, without any sign of life. If we try to burn the branches, we will see that they do not catch fire. Let us double-check that we did not take leafless *yikshat* branches that are alive and full of sap. This time let us make certain we have really dry branches and try again. Now we see that a fire catching the top of one branch does not easily spread to the neighboring branches, and the fire frequently dies out before consuming the available dry wood. It does not seem possible that such a "bramble", which is so difficult to burn, should serve as the metaphor for the threat to the citizens of Shechem: "fire shall come out of the *atad* and consume the cedars of Lebanon." (Nor in the continuation where the moral is given: "Fire will come out of Avimelekh and consume the citizens of Shechem and all Beth-millo, and fire will come out from the citizens of Shechem and Beth-millo and consume Avimelekh." [Judges 9:20])

It is also difficult to accept that Jotham would compare Avimelekh - when the latter is at the height of his power and success - to a drooping bush that has no shade. Such a reading could, perhaps, interpret Jotham's words sarcastically, but then they would lack the wisdom expected of a parable. It is inconceivable that anyone in the audience would have lent his ear or opened his heart to words claiming that this man - selected to rule because of his strength, charisma, and leadership qualities - is nothing but a worthless individual, compared to those crowning him. Such a parable would have insulted those who chose Avimelekh, since it would openly reveal a basic flaw in their judgment. Such a method would not have allowed Jotham to exert any influence on his audience. Yet we know from the Bible that the parable of Jotham had its effect:

> "And the citizens of Shechem rebelled against Avimelekh (and) they set the stronghold on fire and burnt it over their heads, so that all the men of the tower of Shechem died also, about a thousand men and women...[this is the fire that came forth from the *atad*, Avimelekh]...(And) a woman threw a millstone upon Avimelekh's head...(And) the men of Israel saw that Avimelekh was dead... Thus God requited the crime that Avimelekh had committed against his father by the murder of his seventy brothers and

Olive, fig, and grape - Othniel, Deborah, and Barak

The midrash sees in these trees the earlier judges, each one of whom returned to his home and fields after completing the task set him to lead the people in time of trouble. "Jotham spoke a parable. How? 'Once upon a time the trees came' - these are Israel; 'and said to the olive tree' - this is Othniel ben Kanaz [the first judge of Israel]...and what did Othniel say to them? - 'What, leave my rich oil?' They went to Deborah. 'So the trees said to the fig tree' - this is Deborah. She said to them: 'What, leave my good fruit and all its sweetness?'...'So the trees said to the grapevine.' But the grapevine answered: 'What, leave my wine?' The grapevine - this is Barak. And Gideon? 'Rule over us (you, your son and your grandson as well)!' the people said to him. He replied: 'I will not!' Because they saw this was the decision, 'Then all the trees said to the *atad*' - this is Avimelekh. Just as this *atad* is covered with thorns, so Avimelekh is covered with evil deeds...What did he say to them? - 'Come and take refuge in my shade!'" (Midrash Tanhuma, Vayere, 29)

pp. 60-61

The three candidates for kingship
Olive, fig, grapevine

brought all the wickedness of the men of Shechem on their own heads. The curse of Jotham son of Gideon...came home to them."

(Judges 9:23,49-57)

According to the story in the book of Judges, Jotham was wise, seeing what was to befall as a result of Avimelekh's rule, and was even able to shape the events. Avimelekh, on the other hand, at the time of his crowning was immeasurably more powerful than Jotham. So what does the wise man do to disparage the strong man known for his power? Never would he portray him as weak and unimportant. On the contrary, he would publicly acknowledge his strength and charisma, but together with this find a way to reveal weaknesses not immediately apparent, and to present them gradually to the scrutiny and testing of the blinded admirers.

It thus seems that the *atad* in the parable of Jotham cannot be the lowly, shadeless *yikshat* bush, the *Lycium europaeum*. On the contrary, we should search for the *atad* among the **large** trees. It has to be a tree whose height and shade surpass those qualities in the previous candidates for kingship (the olive, fig, and grapevine). The *atad* must also be a fruit-bearing tree whose fruit, however, are not important enough for the tree to reject the kingship because of them. As for fire, its branches must ignite easily and burn so fiercely as to threaten all in the burning *atad*'s vicinity.

All these characteristics are found in the tree called *Ziziphus spina-christi* (L.) Desf. Its identification as the *atad* was strongly supported by Dr. Ephraim Hareuveni. This is a tropical plant that came to Israel from Africa. The *atad* has spread through the length and breadth of Israel's plains. It can be found not only in the Jordan Valley, in the Dead Sea Rift, the Arava and the valleys leading to them, and the Negev, but also in the Jezreel Valley, the coastal plain, and the coastal hills, as well as in places such as the upper reaches of the dry river beds in the vicinity of Shechem. It seems that the *atad* excelled in its growth because its deep and widespread roots take over large growing areas.

In summer and in the first days of the rainy season, the branches abound with small flowers of a greenish-yellow color, with a strong smell that attracts bees, which aid in pollination. The numerous fruit that develop on the tree look like tiny apples. In the Mishna (as generally accepted by both early and late commentators) these fruit were called *rimin* and were listed among the *kalin sh'b'dmai*. (D'mai l,l) The *rimin* are eaten green and taste like a sour apple. When they turn a bright orange or light red, they are sweeter but less juicy than regular sour apples. When they drop from the tree, they taste starchy and are then suitable for boiling into jelly. A hungry passerby with no other food available would be glad to eat the dropped fruit, even raw. Since the *rimin*'s seeds are large, there is little to eat, so the fruit is rarely marketed.

On the other hand, in Arab villages one can sometimes see the domesticated *Ziziphus* (*Ziziphus jujuba* Mill.), whose fruit is larger and sweeter, slightly elongated, and of a darker brownish color. In Arabic these fruit are called *anab*, while in the Mishna they are called *shizafin*. "*Shizafin* and *rimin*, although they resemble each other - it is forbidden to crossbreed them." (Kilaim I,4) The trees do resemble each other closely in their leaves, branches and general shape. But the domesticated *Ziziphus* is less thorny. Since the word *atad* also means "thorn" in Hebrew, it is possible that the name *atad* was given to the thorny tree producing *rimin* fruit in order to distinguish it from its less thorny relative, the *Ziziphus jujuba*, which produces the *shizafin*.

When the *atad*, the *Ziziphus spina-christi*, is left to grow unimpeded, it develops a wide and "wild" look, its foliage made up of clumps that seem to hang in the air. The *atad* is larger than all the other fruit trees native to Israel and casts a wide and heavy shade beneath its boughs. A single full-grown *atad* in a wheat field serves as a cool resting place during harvest time for those working in the field and on the threshing floor, while in grazing areas it offers respite from the sun for shepherds and their flocks. The thorny branches make convenient hangers for hammocks, packs, and overclothes: "Eat the fruit and doze in the shade of the *atad*," says an Arab proverb. Still surviving in Israel are some truly giant-sized *atadim*, such as the one growing near Hatzeva in the Negev. During the days of the Palmach, the armed Jewish force before the establishment of the modern state of Israel, this tree served as a landmark visible from afar for units searching for the spring of water at Hatzeva. An ancient tree that had reached such size was a well-chosen stop in the impressive funeral procession when Jacob's body was brought from the land of Goshen in Egypt to the cave of the Makhpela in Hebron:

> "So Joseph went to bury his father, accompanied by all Pharaoh's courtiers, the elders of his household, and all the elders of Egypt, together with all Joseph's own household, his brothers, and his father's household; only their dependents, with the flocks and herds, were left in Goshen. He took with him chariots and horsemen; they were a very great company. When they came to the threshing-floor of the *atad* beside the river Jordan, they raised a loud and bitter lament, and there Joseph observed the seven days of mourning for his father." (Genesis 50:7-10)

Though the *atad* is beneficial in many ways to shepherds and wheat harvesters, this tree is known to be harmful to fruit trees. It is a strong tree, whose roots spread in a wide circle and compete with the roots of other trees with a vigor the fruit trees cannot rival. A farmer who wants his orchard to succeed must first uproot every *atad* in the vicinity, small saplings as well as full-grown trees.

King of the trees
The ancient atad (Ziziphus spina christi) *in Hatzeva*

63

What is to be done with the uprooted trees? After they dry out, they are chopped up for excellent kindling. Both the thin and the thicker branches quickly catch fire and burn brightly, generating much heat with very little smoke. There is thus a natural association between the *atad* and consuming flames of fire. This is especially true because of other experiences associating fire with the *atad*: Frequently clumps of the *atad*'s branches grow downward, actually reaching the ground. Because of their extreme thorniness (with the base of each leaf having two secondary leaves that turn into thorns: one pointing outward like a javelin and the other bent like a hook), these clumps are not foraged by sheep and goats and the trees continue their thick growth. In order to allow access to the tree trunk (whether for shade or to chop it down), these low-lying branches are sometimes burned as they grow, with the fire consuming all the thin branches and their sharp thorns. It takes little imagination to picture what can happen if such a fire gets out of control...

Familiarity with the *atad* tree explains fully the wisdom of the parable of Jotham: After the trees in search of a king despaired of the goodly fruit-bearing trees, because none was willing to accept the kingship, they all turned to the *atad*. While its fruit are not among the quality fruit (but rather *kalin sh'b'dmai*), its trunk is tall, its foliage is widespread, and it has strength as well as sharp thorns. Although one might disparage the quality of its fruit, Jotham acknowledges the strength of much-admired Avimelekh and his ability to rule. Thus no doubt Jotham succeeds in flattering the judgment of the citizens of Shechem. However, the demand of the *atad* that all the trees "come live in my shade", which seems a logical regal demand, is meant to spark a warning in every farmer familiar with the chances for a fruit tree to develop or even survive in the shade of an *atad* tree.

In the demand "come and live in my shade," Jotham expresses with few words what the prophet Samuel describes at length when he told the people who were asking him for a king:

> "'This will be the sort of king who will govern you,' he said. 'He will take your sons and make them serve in his chariots and with his cavalry, and will make them run before his chariot. Some he will appoint officers over units of a thousand and units of fifty. Others will plough his fields and reap his harvest; still others will make weapons of war and equipment for mounted troops. He will take your daughters for perfumers, cooks, and confectioners, and will seize the best of your wheat fields, vineyards, and olive groves, and give them to his lackeys. Your servants, both men and women, and the best of your cattle and your asses he will seize and put to his own use. He will take a tenth of your flocks, and you yourselves will become his servants."
>
> (I Samuel 8:11-17)

In light of Jotham's warning, even Avimelekh's most ardent admirer could not help but weigh every action Avimelekh took to consolidate his rule.

"If not, fire shall come out of the *atad* and consume the cedars of Lebanon!" With these words, too, Jotham paints a terrifyingly clear picture for the people of Shechem. In order to feel all the might of his words, it is important to remember that the *Ziziphus spina-christi* - the *atad* - grows only in the relatively low places of Israel, not in the mountainous areas. Cedars, on the other hand, grow on the mountain tops of Lebanon. The picture that Jotham draws here is therefore one of fire that will spread throughout the land of Israel: from the valleys, up the hills, and to the mountains of Lebanon. Anyone who has seen an uncontainable forest fire spreading wildly, consuming all in its path, can understand the fear that filled the hearts of the citizens of Shechem when they heard this dire prophecy from Jotham, and how these words influenced their reactions to all the deeds of Avimelekh from the day they anointed him to the day they banded together to betray him.

Mark Antony in the footsteps of Jotham

In world literature there are several examples of this time-tested method. Perhaps the best known is in Shakespeare's play, *Julius Caesar*, Act III, scene 2, in Mark Antony's speech over Caesar's body.

The angry crowd demands to hear from Brutus and Cassius an explanation of Julius Caesar's murder. Brutus addresses the citizens of Rome:

"As Caesar loved me, I weep for him...as he was valiant, I honor him; but as he was ambitious, I slew him...

Citizens: Live, Brutus! Live! Live!..

Third Citizen: Let him be Caesar."

Mark Antony, who has well understood Brutus' cunning words, takes the pulpit to eulogize Caesar. However Mark Antony's true purpose is to expose the real Brutus to the admiring Roman citizenry who now wish to crown Brutus as heir to the murdered Julius Caesar. Mark Antony uses the same method employed by Brutus:

"The noble Brutus hath told you Caesar was ambitious; if it were so, it was a grievous fault, and grievously hath Caesar answered it. Here, under leave of Brutus and the rest, - for Brutus is an honorable man; so are they all, all honorable men, - come I to speak in Caesar's funeral... You all did see that on the Lupercal I thrice presented him a kingly crown, which he did thrice refuse. Was this ambition? Yet Brutus says he was ambitious; and, sure, he is an honorable man..."

And thus Mark Antony continues - with constant reference to Brutus' honor, honesty, and strength - to lead the citizens of Rome step by step towards rebellion against Brutus and his friends, until the enraged cry is heard against Brutus and the rest:

"Fourth Citizen: O traitors! villains!...

Citizens: Revenge! ... Kill! Slay! Let not a traitor live."

The crown of thorns?

The thorny branches of the *atad* tree are considered possible candidates for Jesus' crown of thorns, hence the Latin name, *spina-christi*, "Christ's thorns."

From the viewpoint of the goat
The unsurmountable hedge

Pot, palace, hedge, and kiln

In order to spread a fire, the wind makes use of dry weeds and thorns. One of the outstanding plants that help the wind spread a blaze is a shrub found in many places in Israel, with roots in the Bible and the words of the Sages.

> "It is better to hear the rebuke of the wise, than for a man to hear the song of fools. For as the crackling of the *seerim* under the pot, so is the laughter of the fool."
>
> (Ecclesiastes 7:5-6)

What are these *seerim* whose crackling under the pot on the cooking fire is like the laughter of the fool? Although the Hebrew word *seer* means "pot," most commentators identified the *seerim* as "a kind of thorn." From the several places in the Bible and in the writings of the Sages where *seerim* are mentioned, it is clear that the reference is to a specific thorny plant, not just to "a kind of thorn." This was one of the subjects dealt with by Dr. Ephraim Hareuveni in the early years of his research. He traveled the length and breadth of Israel, studying the various types of kindling commonly used in Arab homes, and the different reactions to fire characteristic of the numerous plants used by the Arabs as kindling. Concomitantly, he researched in the Bible and in the writings of the Sages all the references to *seerim* and *seera*, and concluded that the *seerim* and the *seera* in the Bible and in the language of the Sages are both names for the thorny plant named by Linnaeus, *Poterium spinosum* (from the Greek *poterion*, drinking cup), referred to in modern taxonomy as *Sarcopoterium spinosum* (L.) Sp.

This small plant is very common throughout the hilly regions on both sides of the Jordan (except for regions of basalt rock in the Galilee and wide expanses of the Negev mountains), as well as in the mountains of Lebanon and the anti-Lebanon. From the slopes its seeds are carried down by the runoff waters of the winter rains, enabling the *seerim* shrubs to take root and grow along the dry river beds crossing the coastal plain to the Mediterranean Sea. Indeed, these *seerim* are found along the calcareous sandstone hills of the coastal plain, and occasionally even border the seashore. Here they take on unusual shape and resemble all the other shrubs exposed to the sea winds that sculpt the plants along the shore. The shapes of the *seerim* shrubs vary with their diversified growing regions. In damp and shady areas, the *seerim* have numerous leaves that remain green throughout most of the year. Their stems are soft, the green thorns almost "painless," and the shrubs are big and wide. However, on those slopes exposed to the burning sun and strong winds, the *seerim* are small and remain green only in the latter half of the rainy season. For most of the long months of summer they are almost leafless, brown, hard, and painfully thorny, with the protruding thorns grayish-silver in color.

The *seerim* leaves are subdivided into small leaflets whose beauty can be appreciated only on close inspection. The thorns grow in pairs out of the tips of the branches. Because of this dichotomous branching the shrub takes on a characteristic pillowlike shape. The flowers of the *seerim* are visible primarily at the end of the rainy season and the early part of the summer, although it is possible to see flowering branches in the first days of the rainy season and sometimes even earlier. These flowers have a special beauty revealed only to those who bend down for a close look. Botanists find these flowers of special interest because of their unique structure and their division into male flowers bearing yellow anthers and female flowers bearing red pistils. (There are also *seerim* flowers that contain both anthers and pistils.) Two or three ovaries of each flower are surrounded by four or five sepals joined together to form a small "pot" (*seer* in Hebrew). This little "pot" is green when young, reddish at maturity, and rusty brown in its last stages, when the color is similar to a fired clay pot. The top of the "pot" is covered by the tips of the sepals, which look like a tiny pot cover. This structure gives the plant its name: *seerim* - pots. These little "pots," or compound fruit, are found in numerous quantities on each shrub. They burst in the heat of fire and produce small explosive sounds as they burn:

> "'For as the crackling of the *seerim* under the pot' - said Rabbi Joshua ben Levi [34]: All the trees when they burn do

Jeremiah's real pot

After the identification of the *seerim* shrubs and the resulting explanation of "for the crackling of the *seerim* under the pot," there were those who went so far as to see the *seerim* shrubs in Jeremiah's *seer nafuakh*: "I see a steaming pot *(seer nafuakh)* facing north." (Jeremiah 1:13) There is even a rumor that Ephraim Hareuveni supported this idea. I never heard him say so. More likely, the *seer nafuakh* was a pot on an outdoor stove, with its bubbling contents agitating the pot cover. An opening in the stove gave the wind access to oxygenate the flame. This opening factually faced north, symbolizing that the wind fanning the fire would come from the north: "The evil shall come from the north" (Jeremiah 1:14) - a wind that will fan the flames of war and destruction.

Erosion guards
The Poterium *shrubs protect the slope.*

not produce loud noises, but the *seerim* do, as though saying: 'We too are trees!'"

(Midrash Kohelet Zuta 7,5; in Midrash Kohelet Raba the same words are cited in the name of Rabbi Levi ben Rabbi Zeira.)

From the days of "Kohelet, the son of David, king in Jerusalem" (Ecclesiastes 1:1) who, according to tradition, was King Solomon, to the days of Rabbi Joshua ben Levi, some 1,100 years went by, and more than 1,800 years have passed from Rabbi Joshua ben Levi to our day. Yet today we can still go out to the fields of Israel, gather the *seerim* shrubs and listen to their burning crackle. The likeness will be more complete if we build a clay oven of the kind our ancestors built and place upon it a clay pot containing stew. Then we will really be able to hear "the laughter of the fool" in the flame of the *seerim* as heard by Kohelet ben David in Ecclesiastes and the sounds of the braggart heard by Rabbi Joshua ben Levi.

The sounds produced by the burning *seerim* shrubs occur not only because of the bursting of the fruit in the heat of the fire, but also because of the noise produced by the burning green branches. Such green branches are usually to be found at the base of the shrub even when it appears completely dry. The noisiest "voices" are to be heard when a green *seerim* shrub is set on fire, for then, in early April, it already has red fruit. The ability of the *seerim* shrubs to burn even when they are green, before they have dried in the heat of Israel's summer, can help explain a passage that has confounded scholars for generations:

"Before your pots can feel the thorns, He shall sweep them away as with a whirlwind, both the green and the burning."
(Psalms 58:10, *The Jerusalem Bible* translation)

"All unawares, may they be rooted up like a thorn-bush, like weeds which a man angrily clears away!"
(Psalms 58:9, *The New English Bible* translation)

These diverse translations of the same Hebrew verse are but two examples of the difficulty in understanding this passage in the absence of familiarity with the *seerim* shrub.

The entire psalm deals with the evil of the wicked (probably the wicked judges), who spread wrongdoing and injustice throughout the land. The psalmist beseeches God to destroy the wicked and wipe out their plots, so the righteous can witness the justice of the Lord. The writer of this short psalm makes multiple use of wildlife in his descriptions (the viper, the lion, the snail) so he can illustrate the annihilation that shall befall the wicked even if they are still at the peak of their vitality.

"Before your *seerim* will feel thorny [*atad* in Hebrew], while they are still green, (the Lord) shall sweep them away in a burning whirlwind."
(Psalms 58:10)

On the sea coast
Wind-shaped Poterium *shrubs*

Fire on a rainy day
There is another characteristic apparent when a pile of *seerim* shrubs is set afire: The dry branches catch fire easily, the flame passing through them quickly. At first, very thick white smoke rises from the flame, especially if the pile was compressed before being ignited. The second stage of burning produces heat many times more intense than that of a regular campfire. In addition to the popping noise of the exploding fruit, one can also occasionally hear a peculiar dull roaring sound of the hot wind passing quickly through the air pockets between the branches. The great heat generated by the burning *seerim* can be used on rainy days to dry wet kindling, otherwise not fit for burning. Because of the air spaces between the thin branches, it is easy to dry the *seerim* shrubs themselves if they are placed level with the wind in a sheltered spot such as the entrance to a small cave or beneath a vehicle or even under an *atad* tree.

The psalmist includes the *seerim* shrubs (pulling his audience into personal participation by calling them "**your** *seerim*") by saying that the burning whirlwind will catch the wicked while they are still in the fullness of power, just as the *seerim* shrubs catch fire and are destroyed even while they are still green, before their green branches have turned to thorns. And just as the *seerim* are totally destroyed by fire, so shall the annihilation of the wicked be total. For then "the righteous will rejoice ...(and) men will say, 'there is, then, a reward for the righteous; there is, indeed, divine justice on earth.'" (Psalm 58:11-12)

The fire that catches *seerim* shrubs can spread rapidly along the slopes and hills, igniting fields and forests and consuming everything in its path. This fearful picture is vividly reflected in the pronouncement on Nineveh by the prophet Nahum (Nahum 1). Nahum speaks of the fate God has in store for Nineveh, the capital of Assyria, and its inhabitants. Assyria was a superpower that, during the reign of Hezekiah, king of Judah, towards the end of the eighth century BCE, destroyed many regions in Judah and almost succeeded in capturing Jerusalem. Nahum warns his audience that God's way is to utterly destroy that which He has condemned. This is the way he depicts the terror of God's fire and the flame of revenge of the burning whirlwind, which consumes everything:

> "He rebukes the sea and dries it up,
> And He makes all rivers dry:
> Bashan and Carmel languish,
> And the flower of Lebanon withers.
> The mountains quake because of Him,
> And the hills melt.
> The earth heaves before Him,
> The world and all that dwell therein.
> Who can stand before His wrath?
> Who can resist the flames of His fury?
> His anger pours out like fire,
> And the rocks are broken up by Him."
>
> (Nahum 1:4-6)

Continuing this general description, Nahum paints the frightening picture of fire igniting the *seerim* shrubs, then going on to utterly destroy hills and valleys, spreading further and further destruction, leaving no safe place:

> "He wreaks utter destruction,
> So that affliction will not rise up a second time.
> For (the fire will reach) the tangled *seerim*,
> And while they [the revelers symbolized by the *seerim*] are still drunk,
> They will be consumed utterly like dry straw."
>
> (Nahum 1:9-10)

The fire which caught the Poterium bushes on the forest edge, quickly consumed the entire forest.

"Correction" replaces understanding

Attempts at exegesis of this verse from Nahum show amazing convoluted hypotheses of the commentators and linguists who ignored the natural setting of the prophet's words in the land of Israel. From the ramified literature explaining this verse, we summarize only a few examples from the book by John Smith, Professor of Semitic Languages and Literature at the University of Chicago, published as part of the world-famous series of critical and exegetical commentary, *The International Critical Commentary,* first published by T. & T. Clark in 1911 (fourth impression, 1959). On page 294, Smith states: "As it stands in the Masoretic text, the verse is wholly unintelligible. Modern interpreters have for the most part abandoned it as hopeless and many declare the recovery of the original text impossible." Continuing on pages 301-302, Smith offers suggestions to "alter" or "reconstruct" the verse or parts of it, each suggestion given in the name of the commentator who made it, just as it was written in scientific articles and in exegetic commentaries. The suggestions include totally rewriting the biblical phrases because "the Masoretic text seems to be due to corruption and conflation. It embodies two efforts to restore a corrupt text." Another "correction" changes words because it "presupposes a confusion of (the Hebrew letters) *mem* and *bet*." A third entirely drops words because there was an "unintentional repetition of one or more symbols" in the written word (dittographs).

The weeds of destruction

The description of "*kimos* and *hoah* in its strongholds" provides a complementary parallel to the description of the *seerim* growing and spreading among the palaces. In the opinion of Ephraim Hareuveni, the *kimos* is a member of the *Umbelliferae* family, the *Ammi visnaga* (L.) Lam. This plant quickly spreads over abandoned wheat fields.

Another plant that appears in abandoned fields is a close relative of the *Ammi visnaga*, the *Ammi majus* L. This umbel, bigger and taller than the *kimos*, Ephraim Hareuveni saw as most eligible to be the *kimson*: "I passed by the field of a lazy man, by the vineyard of a man lacking sense. It was all overgrown...with *kimsonim*, and its stone fence lay in ruins." (Proverbs 24:30-31)

The *hoah* too (*Scolymus maculatus* L.) proliferates in abandoned fields and sometimes takes total command of black alluvial soil, saturated with water throughout the winter months. Commenting on the words of Job (31:40) that "*hoah* will grow there instead of wheat", Rabbi Oshaiah [32] said: "This way the Bible teaches you the features of the earth: A field that is covered with *hohim* [plural of *hoah*] is ideal for sowing wheat." (Tanhuma, Re'e, 13) This information clarifies the picture painted by Isaiah in his prophecy of the downfall of Edom: After the conquest of Edom's fortresses, their location will be plowed over into fields. (Compare this to "Zion shall be plowed as a field, and Jerusalem shall become heaps of ruins." Micah 3:12) But these fields will not even yield crops, because they will be abandoned and will yield only *kimos* and *hoah*. This picture vividly reflects the historical enmity between Israel and Edom.

Stunted grapes and stunted belief

Isaiah's parable of the vineyard (chapter 5) is one of the most famous parables in the Bible. It is important to note that "the vineyard of the Lord of Hosts is the house of Israel, and the men of Judah his pleasant plant" was said to people who identified totally with vineyards that they had created and cultivated for generations. The Israelites had cleared forests, built terraces, hoed and weeded, built watchtowers and winepresses. All these labors were etched into the nation's historic memory and were an integral part of their collective experience. However the climax

p. 71

The Poterium bush to the discerning eye
Female Poterium flowers in blossom; new growth of green leaves and thorns from the previous year.
Inset: *Male stamens heavy with pollen*

"Who do you think God is?" asks Nahum of the people of Nineveh from whom "there emerged one who contrives evil against the Lord, a wicked counselor," (Nahum 1:11) who counseled the conquest of Judah. That advice will be overturned, for soon "He will wreak utter destruction" over them and the trouble that will befall them will destroy them in one mighty blow that will not need repeating ("so that affliction will not rise up a second time"). For the flames of His fury will reach the "tangled *seerim*," and when the flames reach them - the evil citizens of Nineveh - His wrath will not be removed until they will be completely consumed at their drunken revels. The great fire will consume them quickly and utterly, just as the tangles of *seerim* burn completely and are destroyed like dry straw that burns in minutes, leaving nothing behind except a few strands of soot blowing in the wind.

The *seerim* are also found in the book of Isaiah in his prophecies of destruction of one of Israel's greatest enemies. In harsh natural imagery - volcanic eruptions, the lives of wild animals, and plants that cover ruins - Isaiah describes the wilderness that will be the inheritance of Edom. Among other things, he says:

> "*Seerim* shall grow up in its palaces,
> *kimos* and *hoah* in its strongholds." (Isaiah 34:13)

The farmer removes the *seerim* from the plowed field and vineyard, leaving them to flourish only in uncultivated areas. But if cultivation ceases and the field goes back to its wild state, the *seerim* shrubs begin to encroach on the abandoned field; in only a few years they take over. Passing through a field or vineyard covered with *seerim* shrubs, one can be sure that the field has not been plowed for several years. Isaiah, when he wants to underscore that the palaces of the Edomites will be utterly destroyed, describes in his vision the *seerim* shrubs that will slowly spread from the uncultivated fields outside the walls into the destroyed city, taking root in the palaces and mansions, where they will flourish forever.

A similar picture is drawn by Isaiah in his "parable of the vineyard" when he wants to describe to his audience what will befall "the vineyard of the Lord of Hosts, the House of Israel":

> "I will remove its thorncover,
> that it may be eaten (by goats);
> I will break through its fence,
> that it may be trampled.
> And I will make it a desolation *[bata]*,
> It shall not be pruned or hoed,

And it shall be overgrown with briars *[shamir]*
and thorns *[shayit].*   (Isaiah 5:5-6)

As we have seen, the *seerim* shrubs take over a vineyard that has ceased
to be cultivated. It seems that this stage of the abandoned vineyard's
takeover by wild plants is called by Isaiah *bata*, desolation, and the
next stage - the ascent of taller and thicker weeds (briars and thorns) -
he calls *shamir* and *shayit*.

Although unnamed, the *seerim* shrubs are also found in the thorncover
in the parable of the vineyard. Today in the Judean mountains and in
villages in Samaria it is still possible to see vineyards enclosed with
stone fences that in turn are topped all along their length with thorny
shrubs. Usually these are *seerim* shrubs, although occasionally other
thorny plants are used. *Seerim* branches intertwine so the wind cannot
easily blow them off the fence, especially when stones are placed over
them to hold them down. They are laid facing outward, thus
preventing goats and sheep from gaining a foothold in the fence to
climb over and ravage the vineyard. This method of protecting a
vineyard clarifies the words of Isaiah: When the thorncover of the
fence is removed, the small cattle (sheep and goats) will be able to jump
over the fence and ravage the vineyard. Later the stone fence itself will
be broken through and the large cattle (cows and oxen) will be able to
amble in and trample what is left underfoot.

The use of such a hedgecover is common not only in vineyards but also
in sheep and goat pens. In this case the shrubs are spread with their
thorns pointing inward in order to prevent the spry goats from
clambering out over the containing fence. This picture from the life of
the flocks is vividly reflected in the words of the prophet Hosea, when
he describes the way of curbing the daughter of Israel when she
wanders off into sidepaths and goes astray:

of the parable bears further consideration:
"He assumed it (the vineyard) would produce
good grapes, but it produced 'bad' grapes *(beushim)*." (verse 2) What are these *beushim*? From
the Mishna (Ma'asrot 1,2) and from the Jerusalem Talmud explaining this Mishna, it is clear
that *beushim* refers to a specific stage of development of the grapes when they cease being embryonic but have not yet ripened. However, there is
a disease that strikes vineyards and prevents the
grapes from ripening, leaving them in the
stunted stage of *beushim*. In modern Israel's vin-
iculture this disease is called *zoteret*, from the

word *zotar*, tiny, since the grape clusters remain
small and stunted. *Zoteret* illuminates the parable: The words of the Bible and the warnings of
the prophets went unheeded, for many in the
kingdoms of Judah and Israel did not perceive
the full meaning of the belief in One God and
remained in the **stunted** stage of growth of "wor-
shipping at both altars" (I Kings 18:21).

The pillar of cloud and the pillar of smoke
Seerim and the *atad* (discussed on pp.59-78) are
found together in a midrash (Tosefta Sota 4,2)
concerning the cloud that went before the Children of Israel in the wilderness during the exodus
from Egypt: "(The cloud) lowers the haughty
and raises the lowly, kills snakes and scorpions,
burns *seerim* and *atad*, and straightens the road
before them (the Children of Israel)." Since *seerim* do not usually grow in the Sinai Desert, from
the context the *"seerim* and *atad"* seem to

represent all the thorny thickets that could have
impeded the Israelites on their way. There is also
a natural association with the pillar of smoke
that rises from the burning *seerim* shrubs.

Briars and thorns
Shamir and *shayit* appear together seven times in
the Bible, all in the book of Isaiah. Three times
the reference is in conjunction with fire that
devours and bursts forth anew:

"Already wickedness has blazed forth like a
fire devouring *shamir* and *shayit*. It has
kindled the thickets of the wood, which have
turned into billowing smoke. By the fury of
the Lord of Hosts the earth was shaken. Next
the people became like devouring fire: no
man spared his countryman."
(Isaiah 9:17-18)

"The Light of Israel will be fire and its Holy
One flame, which will burn and consume its
shamir and *shayit* in a single day, and destroy
soul and body of the glory of its forest and its
vineyards... What trees remain of its forest
shall be so few that a boy may record them."
(Isaiah 10:17...19)

In these descriptions we feel the terror of the fire
burning in the thorns and thistles and quickly
jumping from there to the forest thickets and
destroying them.

Three other times *shamir* and *shayit* are mentioned in Isaiah in one paragraph. As in the parable of the vineyard, here too the picture emerges
of wild plants that take over abandoned vineyards: "For in that day, every place where there
were a thousand vines worth a thousand pieces
of silver shall become a wilderness of *shamir* and
shayit. One will have to go there with bow and
arrows, for the country shall be all *shamir* and
shayit. But the perils of *shamir* and *shayit* shall
not spread to any of the hills that could only be
tilled with a hoe; and here cattle shall be let
loose, and sheep and goats shall tramp about."
(Isaiah 7:23-25) From these verses we learn that
wherever the soil was cultivated ("tilled with a
hoe"), briars and thorns did not hold sway,
while they took hold only in those vineyards that
were not "pruned or hoed." Only once is the
shamir found in Isaiah without the accompany-
ing *shayit*: "My people's soil shall be overgrown
with *kotz - shamir*." (Isaiah 32:13) Here too the
shamir grows on land that has been destroyed
and abandoned; Isaiah added the attribute *kotz*,
the thorn.

Bible study in the field
"For the tangled seerim*...will be consumed utterly
like dry straw."*

A number of commentators have suggested identifying the *shamir* with various plants with similar Arabic names. But none of these suggestions encompasses all the characteristics described above. The Zohary-Feinbrun Israel plant guide identifies *shamir* as the thorny plant, *Paliurus spina-christi* Mill. This same guide, however, confirms that the plant *Paliurus* is rare in Israel. It is therefore illogical that this is the *shamir* that Isaiah portrays as overrunning abandoned vineyards. From all this we do not yet have sufficient information for even tentative identification of the *shamir* and the *shayit*. Yet it is clear that they are thorny wild plants that grow in abandoned vineyards into tangled, tall thickets which serve as hiding places for wild animals; hence the need for "bow and arrows" when entering the thickets.

There is a totally different plant in Israel, in modern Hebrew called *shamir* (from the Arabic *shumar*). This is the fragrant dill that grows along river banks and wadis and in various other habitats; its leaves serve as a marinating spice as well as a common condiment. Dill is a member of the *Umbelliferae* family and has no thorns. It therefore has no connection to Isaiah's *shamir*.

In the *aggada* there is another *shamir*, used to split the stone blocks for Solomon's Temple, so that no metal instrument be used in their dressing. This legendary *shamir* is mentioned in Ezekiel: "But I will make your face harder than theirs, and your forehead stronger than theirs. I will make your forehead like the *shamir*, which is harder than flint." (Ezekiel 3:8-9) This is also mentioned in Zechariah (7:12): "They hardened their hearts like *shamir* against heeding the Torah." What this particular *shamir* is remains a mystery.

The pillar of cloud and the hedgecover
Possibly the words of the Tosefta referred to on p.73 are associated with these words of Hosea. The lesson may be that, so long as the people of Israel obey the Torah, the Lord will "burn *seerim* and *atad* and straighten the road before them." When they abandon the paths of the Torah and worship other gods, God immediately "hedges" their "way with *seerim*."

---

p. 75

The Judean Desert where Saul pursued David
The landscape is dotted with caves which serve as pens for sheep and goats.

"...I will hedge up your way with *seerim*,
And raise fences, and she shall not find her paths."

(Hosea 2:8)

Such stone fences covered with *seerim* bushes (or, where *seerim* are not very plentiful, with other thorny bushes), can still be seen in many regions of the Judean Desert surrounding cave openings that serve as goat and sheep enclosures. It is logical to assume that the compilers of the midrash visualized just such a picture when they imagined the pursuit of David by Saul and Abner in the Judean Desert.

The story in I Samuel is clear:

"And he (Saul) came to the sheepfolds along the way, and there was a cave there, and Saul went in to relieve himself. Now David and his men were sitting in the back of the cave... David went and stealthily cut off the corner of Saul's cloak... Saul left the cave and went on his way. Then David also went out of the cave and called after Saul... 'You can see for yourself now that the Lord delivered you into my hands in the cave today...(yet) I said, "I will not raise a hand against my lord, since he is the Lord's anointed." Please, my dear lord, you can see for yourself: The corner of your cloak is in my hand, but when I cut off the corner of your cloak, I did not kill you...'" (I Samuel 24:3...11)

This biblical story is the basis for the words of the Jerusalem Talmud:

"Why was Abner killed?...And the Sages said: Because he did not allow Saul to be reconciled with David. For it is written: 'Please, my dear lord, you can see for yourself the corner of your cloak in my hand.' Abner replied to Saul: What do you want of your cloak? It was caught by a *seerim* shrub (and tore on the thorns)."

(Jerusalem Talmud, Sota 1,8; Midrash Raba, Bamidbar 19,2)

According to this midrash, Abner did not permit Saul to be reconciled with David. Logic tells us that Abner, commander of Saul's army, must have felt extremely uncomfortable at the implication of his serious neglect of Saul's security in not checking the cave before allowing Saul to enter. So Abner defended himself before Saul by saying David had not been in the cave at all. What happened? The corner of Saul's cloak tore when it caught on the thorns of the *seerim* that covered the fence at the entrance to the cave. The piece of cloth remained fluttering on the thorns and David, who just happened to pass by the same cave, recognized it as part of Saul's cloak and picked it off the *seerim* shrub!

Another major lapse in Abner's security coverage of Saul is recounted in the continuation of the story of Saul's pursuit of David:

"Abner...commander of the army, and Saul lay asleep inside the circle and the troops were posted around him... David and Abishai approached the troops by night and found Saul fast asleep inside the circle, his spear stuck in the ground at his head, and Abner and the troops sleeping around him... David took away the spear and the water skin at Saul's head, and they left. No one saw or knew or woke up; all remained asleep; a deep sleep from the Lord had fallen upon them. David crossed over to the other side and stood afar on top of a hill, a considerable distance between them. And David shouted to the troops and to Abner, 'Abner, are you not going to answer?... You are a man, are you not? And there is no one like you in Israel! So why did you not keep watch over your lord the king?'"

(I Samuel 26:5...15)

The midrash we quoted from the Jerusalem Talmud has this to say:

"Because David and Abishai were able to enter the circle, David said to Abner: 'Abner, are you not going to answer? The corner of the cloak you said had gotten caught on the thorns of the *seerim* shrub. The spear and the water skin, were they too caught on the *seerim* shrub?'"

This midrash does not relate what Abner answered to this sarcastic charge. But in the Babylonian Talmud there is a hint of an answer:

"'Joab [commander of David's forces] left David and sent messengers after Abner, and they brought him back from the cistern of the *seera*.' (II Samuel 3:26) What is the cistern of the *seera*? Said Rabbi Abba bar Kahana [41]: The cistern and the *seera* caused Abner's death."

(Sanhedrin 49a)

Familiarity with the conditions of the Judean Desert enables us to imagine the background for this midrash. Saul, accompanied by many men, had to plan the route of his pursuit of David according to field conditions. He had to ensure rest stops near water cisterns without which such a force could not survive in the desert. It is not difficult to imagine how Abner explained away Saul's spear and the water skin appearing in David's hands. Obviously they did not get "caught on the *seerim* shrub." What then? Probably they were forgotten near the cistern when the troops moved on and later David found them when he went down to the cistern to draw water. From this "the cistern and the *seera* caused Abner's death" - for twice he diverted Saul's heart from David, preventing Saul from believing in David's lack of any evil intent towards his person: once by using the story of the cistern and once with the excuse of the *seerim* shrubs at the entrance to the cave. Therefore it was only poetic justice that Abner be captured by Joab at the "cistern of the *seera*" and then put to death.

The name "cistern of the *seera*" is itself worthy of consideration. It

Shock absorbers and mattresses

During our hikes through the hilly regions of Israel, we have made frequent use of the springiness of the *seerim* shrubs. Many slopes are terraced with natural rocks or with constructed retaining walls. On steep slopes these terrace steps can reach a height of two to three meters or more. It is a special experience to descend such a slope by jumping from terrace to terrace with the help of "shock absorbers" made from *seerim*. The procedure is as follows: At the top of the slope, prepare a large pile of *seerim* shrubs, a minimum of 70-80 centimeters thick after the pile has been thoroughly compressed. Throw this pile on a level spot below the terrace from which the first jump is to be made. The first person jumps and moves aside, to be followed by the equipment of all the hikers. After the first person down has moved all the equipment, the rest of the group jump one by one into the *seerim* pile. Now the pile has to be compressed again and, presto, it is ready to be moved to the next lower terrace to absorb the next series of jumps.

This springiness of the *seerim*, which comes from the pliability of the branches and the dichotomic branching, led to the idea of using *seerim* to prepare mattresses in army training under field conditions. When we first suggested this in officer training courses of the Haganah, the idea was rejected. As I was told, stories about Shadrach, Meshach, and Abednego are fine but don't try to involve them in the daily life of the Haganah training program! Would anyone dream of agreeing to sleep like a fakir on a bed of nails...? Not discouraged, we prepared a supply of *seerim* shrubs, piling thick layers one on top of the other, with their bottom branches facing down. We climbed atop the pile and stamped it down. This stamping broke off most of the thorns; the platform thus created had but to be covered with a blanket or ground sheet to provide outstanding qualities for field conditions: the springiness insulates whoever is lying on such a mattress from cold and damp and protects from pebbles that dig into one's body. Even if the ground gets wet from rain seeping into the tent, the sleeper is protected. And if the camp has to move the following day to a new site, what can be more convenient than to burn the "mattress"

p. 76

Thorns and pots of the Poterium

Young, still-thornless branch (inset) *turns into sharp and spiny thorns* (right).
left
Ripening fruit resemble clay pots. (enlarged tenfold)

to make a hot fire on which to boil water for a hot drink in the cold morning? So from the days of the Haganah and the Palmach till today, many in the Israel Defense Forces and in Israel's youth movements enjoy a good, warm night's sleep during the cold nights, thanks to *seerim* mattresses.

How to drive through mud safely

Another important use of the springiness of *seerim* is to prevent vehicles from sinking in mud. It is a good idea to lay two tracks of compacted *seerim* shrubs along a dirt road (usually muddy in Israel's winter). Each track of *seerim* should be the width of the wheels of the vehicle that has to cross the muddy stretch, with the width between the tracks equal to the vehicle's wheel base. The length of each track must be at least twice the length of the vehicle. When the front wheels reach the forward edge of the *seerim* tracks, each strip should be rolled up like a carpet, cut just behind the rear wheels, and moved ahead of the vehicle, making certain that all four wheels remain on the *seerim* tracks. The two rolls of *seerim* tracks are then spread in front of the vehicle, with the whole process repeated until the dangerous stretch is passed. The slow, hard preventive work is far easier than the chore of extricating a vehicle from deep mud.

How to cool without a cooler

Another pleasant use of the air spaces between the branches of the *Poterium* shrub is as cooling units in summer camps, in army field training exercises, or on hikes. When the *seerim* are wetted with water, and wind passes through the branches, the resulting evaporation causes pleasant cooling. In this way food can be preserved on a hot day or a water tanker cooled to pleasant drinking temperature. In the Ramat Luz Study Center at Neot Kedumim - The Biblical Landscape Reserve in Israel - the roofs are covered with a layer of *seerim* shrubs; sprinklers keep the branches moist on hot days. The result is a marked lowering of inside temperature even during the hottest days of Israel's summer.

---

right
David is the offshoot of an olive
"Your sons are as olive shoots gathered about your table."

p. 79

Saul is the offshoot of a sycamore
The sycamore stump produced three new trunks and one offshoot.

makes sense to assume that this was a lime kiln. Such a kiln is usually built on the slope of a hill in the shape of a round pit. Close to the bottom of the kiln, in the direction of the slope, there is a small opening. The pit is filled with *seerim* shrubs. These are layered with strata of limestone. A fire is kindled in the small opening and the *seerim* in the kiln burn with an extremely hot fire that turns the limestone into quicklime.

The *seerim* shrubs in the lime kiln were also found, it seems, in the midrash on Shadrach, Meshach, and Abednego, who, at the order of Nebuchadnezzar, king of Babylon, were thrust into the fiery kiln from which they emerged hearty and unhurt. (See Daniel 3:19-26.)

> "Said the Sages: On that day six miracles were performed; they are these:...the thorns of the *seera* broke off..."
>
> (Sanhedrin 92,2)

This translation, "the thorns of the *seera* broke off" is by Ephraim Hareuveni. The miracles the midrash lists are in addition to the greatest miracle, namely that the angel of the Lord protected the three from the fiery flames of the kiln. As though that were not sufficient, even the thorns of the *seerim* shrubs, used to fire up the kiln because of their especially hot flame, broke off so that Shadrach, Meshach, and Abednego were not even scratched!

If the Lord of Hosts so protected these righteous men, let us add another comment about His concern for their well-being: Even if the kiln was deep, and even if they were cast in from a great height, we know they would not have been hurt from the fall itself. A thick layer of *seerim (Poterium)* serves as an excellent springy mattress onto which one can fall unhurt from a great height. (see p. 77.)

"As the days of a tree"

Saul and David in the Judean Desert are dominant figures in the stories associated with the *seerim* shrubs. These two leaders, and the differences between them, arise again in references to the olive and sycomore trees of the coastal plain. Among the "stewards of the property of King David" (I Chronicles 27:31) who were responsible for the resources of Israel, Baal-Hanan the Gederite was steward "over the olive trees and the sycomores in the lowlands." (I Chronicles 27:28)

Unlike the olive, the sycomore usually does not grow in mountainous areas; it grows with the olive in the plain. Even today, in the vicinity of Israel's Ben-Gurion Airport, it is possible to see veteran sycomores among the ancient olive trees - specimens of both have hollow trunks with venerable knots. The sycomore has dark green leaves that densely cover the branches, creating a canopy through which bits of sky are visible. The olive tree has dense billowing grayish green foliage that shows a silvery sheen when the wind rustles the leaves. Frequently the olive tree is surrounded by offshoots, the strongest of which are kept by the farmer for transplanting.

In this context it is easy to understand the words of the prophet Isaiah:

> "And a shoot *(hoter)* shall grow out of the trunk of Jesse,
> and a twig *(netzer)* shall sprout from his roots."
>
> (Isaiah 11:1)

The offshoots that surround an olive tree grow both from the roots and the trunk of the tree. When a trunk offshoot grows into a sturdy "branch," it is sometimes cut out from the trunk, together with the

Sycomore not sycamore
The sycomore or Egyptian fig is the *Ficus sycomores* L. It has nothing in common with the American plane tree *(Platanus occidentalis)* nor the English maple *(Acer pseudoplatanus)*, both of which are commonly called sycamore.

"The sign of the lowlands is sycomores"
In contrast to the days of David and Solomon, when the sycomores were plentiful in the plain, the Tosefta (Shvi'it 7,11) attests to the fact that after the wars against the Romans and the suppression of the Bar-Kokhba revolt in the mid-second century CE, the number of sycomores in the plain was drastically reduced. The destruction was so great that Rabban Simeon ben Gamaliel II [19], in trying to establish the sycomore as an "indicator of the lowlands" (see next paragraph), could not supply contemporary corroboration and had to rely on the biblical description: "Simeon ben Gamaliel says: ...the sign of the lowlands is sycomores. And even though we do not have witness to this, there is documentation (in the Bible): 'Cedars (in Jerusalem) as plentiful as sycomores in the lowlands.' (I Kings 10:27)"

Geographical demarcation vs. agricultural demarcation
Students of nature and landscape in Israel are familiar with the Mishnaic determination: "From Kfar Hannania and above (in elevation), everywhere that sycomores do not grow is the Upper Galilee. From Kfar Hannania and below (in elevation), everywhere that sycomores do grow is the Lower Galilee." (Shvi'it 9,2) It is common today to see this statement as a description of the geographical boundaries of the Upper and Lower Galilee. However, it is our opinion that in the context with which the Mishna deals, these do not refer to geographical borders at all but rather to agricultural growing regions that differ in the ripening dates of their fruit: relatively early ripening of fruit in those areas where

p. 80-81

In a plentiful year, the sycomore can provide work for many fig dressers... (see pp.89-92)

p. 82

An ancient sycomore in the Carmel mountains
The Tosefta (Avoda Zara 6,8) mentions a sycomore in the Carmel which was sanctified as a pagan place of worship.

sycomores grow, later ripening of fruit in those areas where sycomores do not grow.

There had to be agreed-upon demarcation for the various regions (each with a different ripening date for its crops) for the purpose of carrying out the injunction of *beu'r*, "clearing out." In the sabbatical year one is allowed to eat "seventh year fruit" in one's home, provided some of these fruit are also left in the field for anyone else, including cattle and other animals. However, when the fruit can no longer be found in the fields, one is not allowed to continue eating them at home unless one performs *beu'r*, the ritual of "clearing out": "He who has fruit from the seventh (sabbatical) year and the time of clearing has come must divide the fruit among his neighbors and relatives and acquaintances by taking them (the fruit) out to the threshold of his home and saying: All Israel are brothers! He who needs to take, let him take! (When this is done) he may return everything (that remains) into his home and eat what remains within his home." (Tosefta Shvi'it 8,2)

But what is "the **time** of clearing"? As stated, this is the time when the fruit disappears from the fields. But because of the wide variety of growing conditions in Israel and the disparity in ripening times in the different regions, the Sages divided the land of Israel into nine regions for the purpose of the injunction of "clearing out."

"There are three districts for *beu'r*: Judea, the east bank of the Jordan, and the Galilee; and (there are) three (regions) within each one." (Shvi'it 9,2) The Galilee was divided into three regions: "Upper Galilee, Lower Galilee and the valley (of the Sea of Galilee)." (Shvi'it 9,2) To clarify that these are not geographical regions but rather agricultural growing regions, the features are underscored: "From Kfar Hannania and above, **everywhere that sycomores do not grow**, is the Upper Galilee." Therefore, if above Kfar Hannania there is a region **where sycomores do in fact grow**, it should be considered similar to the Lower Galilee for the purpose of affixing the ripening date for fruit for the "time of clearing" *(beu'r)*. Similarly, "from Kfar Hannania down, **wherever sycomores do grow** is the Lower Galilee." From this we learn that in any region of the Lower Galilee, **where sycomores do not grow**, the "hour of clearing" is on the same date as in the Upper Galilee.

p. 85

"The produce of the sanctified trees is forbidden."
Ripe sycomore fruit grow on branchlets protruding from the trunk.

thickened growth at the point of attachment. It is then smoothed and worked into a staff with a thick knob at its head - the *hoter*, or shepherd's staff. It serves the shepherd both as a weapon and as a tool for directing the flock. To keep the sheep and goats walking in the desired direction, the shepherd will throw this staff ahead of the flock, for it will always land on its heavier head. This use is reflected in the midrashic expression: "Throw the *hoter* in the air and it will land on its base." (Yalkut Shimoni, Vayeshev 145, and other places.)

Unlike the *hoter*, worked from the offshoot that grows from the trunk of the olive tree, the *netzer* is an offshoot that grows from the roots of the tree. The olive grower destroys most of these offshoots, leaving only one or two of the sturdiest to develop into new saplings for transplant. This is the guarded offshoot [the word *netzer* being derived from the Hebrew word *natzor*, to guard], selected from among all the others to propogate the new generation of olive trees. This becomes a beautiful symbol in Psalm 128: "Your sons are like olive saplings around your table." (128:3)

These characteristics of the olive offshoots help explain the words of Isaiah (in 11:1) which describe the Messiah, a descendant of David, son of Jesse, who will be a leader of his flock (represented by the *hoter*, the shepherd's staff with which he leads his flock) and who will grow as the guarded sapling (the *netzer*) from the roots of the stock of Jesse. Though that ancient stock was chopped down during the destruction of the Temple, the roots did not lose their ability to put forth the new growth of a fruitful tree.

Occasionally one can also find offshoots around a sycomore, especially around the stump of what was a "virgin" sycomore. However, these are not normally used for the cultivation of new trees. Sycomore tree breeding is done by planting cuttings taken from young branches. This is illustrated in a colorful midrash that has its roots in the experience and tradition of many generations. The Bible recounts:

> "In David's reign there was a famine that lasted year after year for three years. So David inquired of the Lord and He answered: 'Blood-guilt rests on Saul and on his family because he put the Gibeonites to death.'" (II Samuel 21:1)

Why did the Lord bring the punishment of famine in the days of David when the sin was committed by King Saul? To this Rabbi Huna (bar Avin) [52] replied in the name of Rabbi Samuel bar Rav Isaac [48]:

> "Because Saul was an offshoot of a sycomore he could not withstand it (the famine), so the Lord passed the famine on to David who was an offshoot of an olive tree and (therefore) could withstand it." (Ruth Raba, 1; Breshit Raba 25)

Indeed the usefulness of a sycomore offshoot is very limited because it withers soon after being removed from the tree. This is the reason why the sycomore offshoot is not normally used to plant a new tree. Saul

84

did not, in fact, found a dynasty in Israel. David did. David was the olive tree offshoot that, after being planted, grew into an olive tree of great age. Moreover, the olive offshoot can survive for days after being severed from the parent tree, even without soil or water. This characteristic was used by the compiler of the midrash to explain why King David, being an olive tree offshoot, could withstand a lengthy famine. Saul, on the other hand, being a sycamore offshoot, could not survive the deprivation.

The form of the figure of speech is noteworthy - metaphor rather than simile. Saul **was** an offshoot of the sycamore (not "like" a sycamore offshoot, nor "compared to" a sycamore offshoot). David, too, **was** an olive tree offshoot. The identification of the characters with the trees is unreserved, a statement of obvious and recognized fact.

The identification of Saul of the tribe of Benjamin with an offshoot of a sycamore brings us to the tribe of Benjamin itself and its figurative relationship to this tree. The men of the tribe of Benjamin were superb soldiers and fighters. In the war of annihilation, declared upon Benjamin by all the other tribes of Israel because of the deeds over the concubine in Gibeah (see Judges 19-21), Benjamin was outnumbered fifteen to one! Yet the men of the other tribes of Israel succeeded in overcoming the Benjaminites only by ruse, deception and ambush, and not in face-to-face combat. The tribe of Benjamin was almost totally destroyed in this war, except for 600 men who fled to the Rock of Rimon. (Judges 20:47)

Despite this near mortal blow, the tribe of Benjamin exhibited unimaginable vitality. Not only was the tribe not eradicated nor assimilated into the other tribes of Israel, it regenerated itself quickly and became foremost among the tribes - so much so that the first king of all Israel, Saul, came from the tribe of Benjamin.

Similar extraordinary regenerative powers are an outstanding characteristic of the sycamore tree. Even if chopped down at ground level, it will restore itself and grow new limbs. If the wind carries away the sand and bares the sycamore's roots, the tree will grow deeper roots and fasten them firmly in the ground. Even if the sands cover the sycamore, branches and all, still it will survive. The branches will produce roots extending into the sand and new growth extending upward out of the sand, so that in a short time, a young and vigorous tree will be visible above ground. In Hebrew, the very name of the sycamore, *shikma*, is related to the word *shikum*, meaning rejuvenation, the most outstanding trait of the sycamore.

It is likely that the Sages' identification of Saul with a sycamore offshoot stemmed not only from the inability of the sycamore offshoot to develop into a tree, but also from the identification of the entire tribe of Benjamin with the sycamore: As the sycamore, so the tribe - both stand out in their ability to grow anew, not from an offshoot but from the trunk.

p. 86

"Like this sycamore that survives in the earth for 600 years."

top
A sycamore covered over with sand grows anew.
bottom
Even when the sycamore's roots have been exposed, they continue to reach for "footholds" in the sand.

Recognition of this ability also helps in understanding the midrash based on Isaiah's prophecy:

"Men shall build houses and live to inhabit them,
Plant vineyards and eat their fruit;
They shall not build for others to inhabit
Nor plant for others to eat,
For as the days of a tree shall be the days of My people..."

(Isaiah 65:21-22)

"'As the days of a tree shall be the days of My people,' like this sycomore that survives in the earth for 600 years."

(Breshit Raba 12,6)

Two questions arise. First, does the sycomore live **only** 600 years? Second, if so, would the Sages have compared the people of Israel to a tree having a known, limited lifespan?

Familiarity with the sycomore's ability to grow anew even after being completely buried in the sand, clarifies the term "in the earth" not as an indication of the tree's lifespan but rather as an expression of the sycomore's ability to survive under the earth for an extended time - until the conditions are right for it to produce visible new growth. This explanation is also in harmony with Isaiah's description (in 65:21-22) of the regeneration of the people of Israel after years of exile.

Food for the king's table
The division of the land of Israel into different growing regions, with varying ripening dates of produce, was already done, it appears, by King Solomon: "Solomon had twelve regional overseers over Israel and they supplied the food for the king and the royal household, each being responsible for one month's provision in the year." (I Kings 4:7) The names of the overseers follow, with references to the tribes they represented and the regions they commanded. A glance at a suitably marked map shows that these regions were not the same as the boundaries of the tribes of Israel. This led various commentators to far-fetched conclusions concerning changes perpetrated over the centuries in the regions allotted to each tribe, or to the existence of covenants between various tribes. However, anyone familiar with nature in Israel can immediately see that these twelve regions match the different **growing** regions of Israel. Division along these lines enabled the regional overseers to "supply the food for the king and the royal household" - each one in the month assigned to him - and to bring foods that were out of season in the other regions. This further enhanced the prestige of the king in the eyes of foreign guests. This, indeed, is the description of Rabbi Hama ben Hanina [39]: "They would bring him (Solomon) chard in summer and squashes in the rainy season." (Dvarim Raba 1,5)

Intimation of the 600 survivors
Perhaps the number 600 in the midrash also hints at the 600 of the tribe of Benjamin who survived the slaughter after the war over the concubine in Gibeah.

The prophet
and the sycomore

The speedy regeneration of the sycomore was utilized by the Israelites to grow building material. The importance of the sycomore in building is attested to primarily in the Mishna and the Tosefta. To get as many construction beams as possible from one sycomore tree, the common practice was to cut down a "virgin" tree, which develops a good-sized trunk after a few years of growth. From the stump that was left, multiple new limbs would then grow. These were used for building material, with yet another generation of new limbs growing out from the recut stump. Cutting the virgin sycomore was therefore considered agricultural work and forbidden during the sabbatical year, because its intent was to produce repeated yields of sycomore tree limbs.

> "One does not cut down a virgin sycomore in the sabbatical year because this is (agricultural) work."
>
> (Shvi'it 4,5)

And also:

> "If one rents a field for only a few years, one is not to sow flax nor cut down sycomore limbs. If one rents for seven years, in the first year one may sow flax and cut down sycomore limbs."
>
> (Baba Metzia 9,9)

From this rabbinical ruling we learn that the Israelites used sycomore limbs only after the tree had a chance to grow for a minimum of six years. For this reason, the lessee could make use of sycomores in a leased field only if the lease was signed for a minimum of seven years and the sycomore limbs were cut down in the first year of the lease. This insured that when the field reverted to the original owner, new

What is the virgin sycomore?
The definition of a "virgin sycomore" is found in the Tosefta (Shvi'it 3,14-15): "There are three (types of) virgins: the virgin girl, virgin soil, and the virgin sycomore. The virgin girl - who has never known a man. Virgin soil - which has never been worked. (Rabban Simeon ben Gamaliel [19] says: Soil in which pottery fragments are not found. [In this, Rabban Shimon ben Gamliel predates modern archeology by many centuries!]) Virgin sycomore - a (sycomore) tree that has never been cut down."

limbs would have already grown from the sycomore stumps, reaching the size of the earlier generation that had been cut down by the lessee.

The importance of sycomore trunks becomes apparent from the following incident in the Tosefta:

> "Abba Saul [18] says: There were sycomores in Jericho that were (cut down and) taken by robbers. Therefore, their owners sanctified them to the Lord."
>
> (Tosefta Menakhot 13,20; Tosefta Zevakhim 11,17)

In this way the owners put a stop to the robbery, for even robbers in those days did not dare touch trees sanctified to God. Obviously though, this same sanctification prevented the owners themselves from making use of the sycomore limbs. However a question arose concerning the legality of enjoying the sycomore **fruit**:

> "The people of Jericho did six things. Three of these were uncontested [by the Sages of Jerusalem] and three were contested...and these are the ones that were contested: permission to use the sanctified branchlets *(gamziot)*...of the sycomore."
>
> (Pesahim 4,8)

And the Tosefta explains:

> "They told them [the Sages of Jerusalem to the people of Jericho]: Do you not accept that the produce of sanctified trees is forbidden (for use)? They replied [the people of Jericho to the Sages of Jerusalem]: Our fathers sanctified only the limbs themselves because robbers came and took them by force."
>
> (Tosefta Pesahim 2,22)

As was explained by Ephraim Hareuveni [*The Gamziot*, "Leshonenu," vol. 11, booklet 1, 1941.], *gamziot* was the name given to the thin branchlets on which the sycomore fruit grow. These branchlets grow on the trunk and limbs of the sycomore in tight clusters, with the fruit developing at the tips. This explains the case presented by the people of Jericho. They claimed that the sanctification was limited to the **limbs** of the sycomores and did not apply to the branchlets growing out of these limbs, and all the more so did not apply to the fruit growing from the tips of these branchlets!

This story documents the great importance of sycomore cultivation in the Valley of Jericho both for building material and for the sweet fruit.

The cultivation of sycomores in Jericho may, perhaps, explain the background for the actions of Amos (the prophet from Tekoa in the southern kingdom of Judah) in Beth-El in the northern kingdom of Israel.

Amos, who was "among the herdsmen of Tekoa" (Amos 1:1), must have followed the practice of other shepherds of the area. At the end of the dry, hot summer, when all the pasturage was gone from the Judean

Desert, he would move his herds of goats and sheep to the Jordan Plain in the Jericho Valley. This is an area rich in green forage throughout Israel's scorching summer season. This is the season when unripe sycomore fruit cover the tips of the branchlets. These embryonic fruit must be pierced (a process called *blissa* in Hebrew) and wiped with oil. This care is needed if the fruit is to reach juicy ripeness. It is not practicable in today's agricultural industry to invest the manual labor and time needed for *blissa* to ensure a harvest of top-grade sycomore fruit; therefore the fruit is not marketed. However, this was not the case in the days of Israel's ancient agriculture:

> "Embryonic (sycomore) fruit may be pierced and oiled until Rosh Hashana." (Shvi'it 2,5)

Unlike the fig, which ripens throughout the summer, the embryonic sycomore fruit develops on many trees only at the end of summer, ripening in autumn. The piercing, frequently accompanied with oiling of the fruit, was therefore considered in the Mishna as work that was permitted on the "eve" of the sabbatical year (the sixth year of the "week of years") right up to the start of the sabbatical year on Rosh Hashana. This, despite the fact that the fruit ripens only after the onset of the sabbatical year itself.

The appropriate season for piercing the sycomore fruit, at least for the sycomores growing in the Jericho Valley, was around the time when the shepherds descended from the desert slopes of Judea and Samaria into the valley. Flocks could graze in the valley, while the shepherds could "moonlight" at other jobs. It is reasonable to assume that the sycomore owners utilized this convenient fact to offer grazing rights in exchange for dressing the sycomore fruit. The shepherd could perch on the sycomore's broad branches and keep a lookout over his flocks while doing the monotonous work of piercing and oiling the still-green fruit. The sycomore owners, on the other hand, were assured of a top-grade crop.

Imagine the meeting between the shepherds from Beth-El, in the hills of Ephraim in Israel, and Amos from the hills of Tekoa in Judah. Listen, if you will, to the complaints of the shepherds from Beth-El as they sit on the limbs of a large sycomore tree together with Amos and tell him the bitter fate of the poor and downtrodden in the kingdom of Israel. Amos listens and the wrath of the Lord fills his heart. He asks one of the other shepherds to watch over his flocks while he, filled with righteous anger, goes up to Beth-El, but one day's walk from Jericho. In Beth-El he warns against oppression and injustice: "They sell the innocent for silver and the destitute for a pair of shoes." (Amos 2:6) This infuriates Amaziah, the priest of Beth-El, who rebukes Amos sharply: "Be off, you seer! Off with you to Judah! You can eat your bread and do your prophesying there." (Amos 7:12) In other words, Amos is to earn his living through prophecy only in the kingdom of Judah, not here in the kingdom of Israel. To this Amos replies:

> "I am not a prophet, nor am I a prophet's disciple; I am a herdsman and a dresser of sycomore fruit. The Lord took me as I followed the flock and said to me: 'Go and prophesy to My people Israel.'"
>
> (Amos 7:14-15)

Thus does Amos clarify to Amaziah and all in hearing that he is not one of those "prophets" who sell their "prophecies" to any buyer, shaping their visions according to the desires of the customer. Amos is not a "professional" prophet; he does not earn his living from prophecy, nor does he ask the people of Beth-El for any payment. He came to say what had to be said as a messenger of the Lord, to return at the end of his mission to the livelihood awaiting him - shepherding and the piercing of sycomore fruit.

The sycomore helps the short tax collector
Just as Rabban Simeon ben Gamaliel [19] had no contemporary corroboration of sycomore trees as an "indicator of the lowlands," so too we have no contemporary corroboration of widespread sycomore cultivation in Jericho. Today sycomores have been replaced by various tropical fruit trees that require far less work than the sycomores to produce good yields. At any rate, confirmation of the sycomores in Jericho during the Second Temple period can be found in the Gospel of Luke: "Entering Jericho he (Jesus) made his way through the city. There was a man there named Zacchaeus; he was superintendent of taxes and very rich. He was eager to see what Jesus looked like; but, being a little man, he could not see him for the crowd. So he ran ahead and climbed a sycomore tree in order to see him, for he was to pass that way." (Luke 19:1-3)

Sycomore fig dressing was researched by Professor Yaakov Galil of Tel Aviv University and his assistants. Their research results were published in *Teva V'aretz*, vol.8, booklets 9,10,11, 1966.

"The king made...cedars as plentiful as sycomores in the lowlands"

In comparison to beams of other trees, sycomore beams are rather light and are impervious to rot for many years. Egyptian sarcophagi made of sycomore wood have been found in perfect state of preservation. It is not surprising, therefore, that *halakha* views the sycomore as an equal of the cedar, and even preferable to the cedar in certain circumstances. For instance, in this rabbinical ruling dealing with everyday life:

> "One who has rented a house and it collapsed, must rebuild it. If it was roofed with cedars, one is not to roof it with sycomores; if it was roofed with sycomores, one is not to roof it with cedars." (Tosefta Baba Metzia 8,32)

And relating to the renovation of a dilapidated two-story house:

> "If the tenant of the ground floor...wants to replace a ceiling with cedars - he is permitted; if with sycomores - he is not... If the tenant of the upper floor wants to replace...his roof with cedars he is not permitted; if with sycomore, he is." (Baba Metzia ll7b)

From these examples it is clear that the rabbis' judgments regarding cedars and sycomores as building materials were based on practical considerations and not prestige. For instance, in the case of the two-story dilapidated house, the tenant of the upper story is permitted to build with sycomore wood rather than the original cedar wood because sycomore wood is lighter and lessens the danger of collapse.

From all the preceding, one may deduce that Baal-Hanan the Gederite, appointed by King David as steward "over the olive trees and the sycomores in the lowlands," was probably responsible for the yields of olive oil and olives and the piercing of the sycomore fruit in season, as well as the orderly cutting of the virgin sycomores and the production of sycomore beams and their proper use.

Despite the importance of sycomore beams for building material, it is apparent that imported cedars, and not the local sycomores, betokened David's rise in status and wealth after he captured Jerusalem and established it as his capital:

> "King Hiram of Tyre sent envoys to David with cedar logs, carpenters, and stonemasons; and they built a palace for David. Thus David knew that the Lord had established him as king over Israel and had exalted his kingship for the sake of His people Israel."
> (II Samuel 5:11-12)

In the version given in I Chronicles (22:4), David also prepared cedar wood, among the other building materials he gathered together in Jerusalem, for the building of the Holy Temple.

However, the king who brought the most cedar trees and wood to Jerusalem was Solomon, David's son.

> "Then Solomon resolved to build a House for the Lord and a royal palace for himself. Solomon engaged seventy thousand porters and eighty thousand quarriers in the hills, with three thousand six hundred men supervising them. Solomon sent this message to King Hyram of Tyre: 'In view of what you did for my father David in sending him cedars to build a palace for his residence, now I intend to build a House for the Lord my God...Send me cedars, juniper [*brosh* in the Hebrew original], and algum wood from the Lebanon, for I know that your servants are skilled at cutting the trees of Lebanon. My servants will work with yours to provide me with a great stock of timber; for the House which I intend to build will be singularly great. I have allocated for your servants, the woodcutters who fell the trees, twenty thousand *kor* of crushed wheat and twenty thousand *kor* of barley, twenty thousand *bat* of wine and twenty thousand *bat* of oil.'

> "Hyram, king of Tyre, sent Solomon this written message in reply: 'Because the Lord loved His people, He made you king over them... We undertake to cut down as many trees of Lebanon as you need, and deliver them to you as rafts by sea to Jaffa; you will transport them to Jerusalem.'"
> (II Chronicles 1:18, 2:1-3,7-10,15)

Expensive import
Kor and *bat*: According to W.F. Albright, as cited in the *Encyclopaedia Judaica*, v.16, p.380, one *kor* is equivalent to 220 liters and one *bat* to 22 liters. In other words, King Solomon annually sent King Hiram four million four hundred thousand (4,400,000!) liters each of wheat and barley and four hundred and forty thousand (440,000) liters each of olive oil and wine!

Identification uncertain
Although the name *brosh* appears in the Bible many times and is described as having a number of uses, there is no consensus as to its identification. Clearly, it was widely used in construction and manufacture. A more exact identification may be feasible when it becomes possible to inspect other trees growing in the mountains of Lebanon and to study all the uses to which the different trees are put. It is likely, though, that the *brosh* is the juniper, and the *te'ashur*, mentioned later in this chapter, the cypress.

p. 95

"The righteous man flourishes like a date palm, grows tall as a cedar of Lebanon."
Date palms and cedars are reflected in the "Pool of Solomon" at Neot Kedumim. (see p. 100)

pp. 96-97

Cedars of Lebanon transplanted from Jersualem thrive at Neot Kedumim.

94

These passages describe a detailed long-term trade agreement of broad scope between King Solomon and King Hiram of Tyre that enabled Solomon to bring to Jerusalem from Lebanon quantities of cedar and juniper *(brosh)* for construction, roofing, and paneling in the Holy Temple, in his palace, in the "House of the Forest of Lebanon," and in his other mansions.

> "The king made silver as common in Jerusalem as stones, and cedars as plentiful as sycomores in the lowlands."
>
> (I Kings 10:27)

Could King Solomon, the wisest of men, who spoke "of trees, from the cedar of Lebanon to the hyssop that grows in the rock" (I Kings 5:13), not have known that the sycomore, which was so plentiful in Israel, was as good a building material as the cedar? Could Solomon, who married Pharaoh's daughter, not have known that the Egyptians used sycomore wood for the construction of their sarcophagi because this wood does not rot? Why then did Solomon go to so much trouble? Why did he incur such heavy payment and dispatch so many men to work far from home?

Truly there is nothing like a cedar "with fair branches, shade giving, towering high" (Ezekiel 31:3) that "grew taller than any other tree, its boughs were many, its branches spread far; for water was abundant in the channels...and in its shadow all great nations made their home." (Ezekiel 31:5-6) The cedar symbolized strength and height, glory and wealth. Not so the sycomore, which does not have an imposing crown such as the cedar, nor does it grow to the great height of over thirty meters that a cedar can attain after many years.

Solomon's decision to import cedars from Lebanon, instead of using the local, plentiful sycomores, came from his desire to raise the prestige of Jerusalem above that of all other nations. This ambition to increase the capital's glamour and majesty is reflected in the descriptions of treasures which flowed into Jerusalem during Solomon's reign, and in the emphasis on the uniqueness of the products made from these materials. Here are but a few examples:

> "Hiram's fleet, which carried gold from Ophir, brought in from Ophir a huge quantity of *almog* wood and precious stones. The king used the *almog* wood for decorations in the House of the Lord and in the royal palace, and for harps and lyres for the musicians. Such *almog* wood has never arrived since or been seen to this day." (I Kings 10:11-12)

> "The servants of Hiram and the servants of Solomon who brought gold from Ophir, brought *algum*-wood and precious stones. The king made of the *algum*-wood ramps for the House of the Lord and for the royal palace, and for the musicians lyres and harps whose like had never before been seen in the land of Judah." (II Chronicles 9:10-11)

Almog: coral or wood?

Many commentators believe that *almog* wood (or *algum* wood as it appears in the version in II Chronicles) is not a tree at all but rather coral (*almog* in modern Hebrew). In the Babylonian Talmud (Rosh Hashana 23a, Baba Batra 80b) the translation of *almog*, according to the tradition brought to Israel by Rav Dimai [49], is *cassita*. From the description of the gathering of this *cassita* from the sea it is clear that the reference is to sea coral:

> "They bring there 6,000 men for twelve months and load the boat with sand until it sinks down. Then a diver goes down and ties a rope of flax to the coral *(cassita)* while the other end is tied to the boat. The sand is then taken and thrown overboard, and as the boat rises it pulls the coral up with it. The coral is worth twice its weight in silver. There were three ports, two belonging to the Romans and one belonging to the Persians. From the Roman side they brought up coral *(cassita)*; from the Persian side pearls *(marganita)*."
>
> (Rosh Hashana 23a)

It is worth noting that today too the shores of the Mediterranean Sea are rich in red coral, especially the shores of Algiers, Tunisia, southern Spain, Provence, Sardinia, Corsica, Sicily, and the Bay of Naples.

The Midrash Hagadol (Truma 25,10) states: *"Almogim - morgana."* Rambam [62] too (in his commentary to the Mishna, Kelim 13) says: *"Almog - almarg'an,* and this is a plant that grows on the sea bed... It is soft before it is exposed to air and then becomes hard like rock..." In fact, one of the Arabic names for coral is *almarg'an* - a word reminiscent of the Latin for pearl - *margarita,* which also comes from the sea. According to the description cited above from the Tractate Rosh Hashana, there was a distinction, it would seem, between *almogim* of the *cassita* variety and *almogim* of the *marganita* or *margerita* variety.

Despite these traditions, the Jerusalem Talmud (Ketubot, end of chapter 7) and midrashim from Breshit Raba (Parasha 15a) cite the tradition that identified the *almog* as aloe. This is consi-

p. 98

Sycomores and cedars planted at Neot Kedumim.

dered to be the *Aquilaria agallocha*, native to India, and used for different wood products as well as for perfume production. Others identify *almog* as a low-growing tree of the legume family (*Pterocarpus santalinus* L., called in Arabic *sandal* or *sandalan*), a heavy dark red wood that is used as a dyestuff - red sandalwood.

It thus appears that our information is as yet insufficient for a positive identification of *almog* or *algum*. It may be corals torn from their reef in the western Mediterranean Sea and brought to Israel in the "Tarshish fleet," or perhaps wood brought from distant lands and sold by the Sidonians (which would explain Solomon's request of King Hiram to "send me cedars, juniper and *algum* wood from the Lebanon"). Or perhaps the two are totally different and the *algum* in II Chronicles is wood, while the *almog* in I Kings is coral. In any case, one thing is clear: The Bible unquestionably is speaking of the import of valuable and prestigious articles from which Solomon ordered decorations and musical instruments to be made "whose like had never before been seen in the land of Judah."

King Solomon as a landscape architect

The Hebrew use of the plural form for "planted" and "flourish" strongly indicates that the reference is not only to a comparison between the righteous man and cedars and date palms, but to the actual, physical presence of these trees in the courtyard of the Holy Temple in Jerusalem.

"The king also made a large throne of ivory, and he overlaid it with refined gold. Six steps led up to the throne, and the throne had a back with a rounded top, and arms on either side of the seat. Two lions stood beside the arms, and twelve lions stood on the six steps, six on either side. No such throne was ever made for any other kingdom."

(I Kings 10:18-20)

In light of all the efforts to create artifacts in Jerusalem "whose like had never before been seen in the land of Judah," and that had never been made in "any other kingdom," it is easy to assume that Solomon brought from Lebanon not only cedar wood for building material but also **cedar saplings** for planting. And just as he appointed "twelve regional overseers" who each provided food for the king and his household during a specific month of the year (I Kings 4:7), so Solomon also, we may assume, knew how to dazzle "all the kings of the earth (who) came to pay homage" (II Chronicles 9:23) with splendid gardens in which were planted together cedars from the snow-covered mountains of Lebanon and date palms from the burning desert. This juxtaposition of vistas is clearly reflected in the words of the psalmist:

"The righteous man flourishes like a date palm,
grows tall as a cedar of Lebanon,
planted in the house of the Lord,
they flourish in the courts of our God." (Psalms 92:13-14)

Aside from the exceptional beauty achieved by this landscaping, it is also possible to see a symbolic expression of the patronage that Solomon extended to the neighboring kingdoms, as is written: "For he controlled the whole region west of the Euphrates - from Tiphsah to Gaza - and he had peace on all his borders round about." (I Kings 5:4)

Solomon's greatness, his majestic construction work in Jerusalem, and his extraordinary gardening projects are also reflected in the tradition ascribing to him "the words of Kohelet, son of David, king in Jerusalem" (Ecclesiastes 1:1):

"I multiplied my possessions. I built myself houses and I planted vineyards. I laid out gardens and groves, in which I planted every kind of fruit tree. I constructed pools of water to irrigate a forest springing up with trees... Thus I gained more wealth than anyone before me in Jerusalem."

(Ecclesiastes 2:4-6,9)

All this, the Bible tells us, was not enough. For even "the palanquin that King Solomon had made for himself was of wood from Lebanon" (Song of Songs 3:9); and as if even this were not sufficient, he built a special building out of cedar wood, the "House of the Forest of Lebanon:"

"For he built the house of the forest of Lebanon: the length thereof was a hundred cubit, and the breadth thereof fifty cubits, and the height thereof thirty cubits, upon **four** rows of cedar pillars, with cedar beams upon the pillars. And it was covered with cedar above upon the side chambers, that lay on forty and five pillars, fifteen in a row. And there were **beams** in three rows; and **light was over against light in three ranks.** And all the doors with their posts were square in the frame and **light was over against light in three ranks.**" (I Kings 7:2-5, *The Jewish Publication Society* translation)

"He built the House of the Forest of Lebanon; its length was a hundred cubits, and its breadth fifty cubits, and its height thirty cubits, and it was built upon **three** rows of cedar pillars, with cedar beams upon the pillars. And it was covered with cedar above the chambers that were upon the forty-five pillars, fifteen in each row. There were **window frames** in three rows, and **window opposite window in three tiers.** All the doorways and windows had square frames and **window was opposite window in three tiers.**" (I Kings 7:2-5, *Revised Standard Version* translation)

The striking differences between these two translations of the original Hebrew description of the House of the Forest of Lebanon are an example of the confusion caused by the seeming obscurity of the Hebrew text. (For those readers interested in comparing the original to the translations, the Hebrew text is given in the margin.)

The unusual name, the "House of the Forest of Lebanon," aroused the interest of many commentators and researchers who attempted to work out the difficulties inherent in the biblical description of this building. The very name, "House of the Forest of Lebanon," was translated by Jonathan (compiler of the first known translation of the Bible into Aramaic around the first century CE) as "the king's cool house" (summer palace). Radak [63] explains: "It seems that the practice of kings in those days was to build houses in the forest to cool off in summer." Many followed this elucidation and there were even those who maintained that the "summer house" was actually built in the mountains of Lebanon and not in Jerusalem. Others were certain that the name was given because it was built on cedar pillars. But why would Solomon use such a pretentious name for a house built on a few dozen cedar pillars?

We believe Solomon used a sophisticated gimmick to create for the visitor the illusion that he was in some kind of forest rather than in a simple pillared hall. To achieve such an illusion it would be necessary to make the pillars look like actual trees, and for these few dozen "trees" to become a "forest."

"וַיִּבֶן אֶת-בֵּית יַעַר הַלְּבָנוֹן מֵאָה אַמָּה אָרְכּוֹ וַחֲמִשִּׁים אַמָּה רָחְבּוֹ וּשְׁלֹשִׁים אַמָּה קוֹמָתוֹ, עַל אַרְבָּעָה טוּרֵי עַמּוּדֵי אֲרָזִים וּכְרֻתוֹת אֲרָזִים עַל-הָעַמּוּדִים. וְסָפֻן בָּאֶרֶז מִמַּעַל עַל-הַצְּלָעֹת אֲשֶׁר עַל-הָעַמּוּדִים אַרְבָּעִים וַחֲמִשָּׁה, חֲמִשָּׁה עָשָׂר הַטּוּר. וּשְׁקֻפִים שְׁלֹשָׁה טוּרִים וּמֶחֱזָה אֶל-מֶחֱזָה שָׁלֹשׁ פְּעָמִים. וְכָל-הַפְּתָחִים וְהַמְּזוּזוֹת רְבֻעִים שָׁקֶף, וּמוּל מֶחֱזָה אֶל-מֶחֱזָה שָׁלֹשׁ פְּעָמִים" (מלכים א ז', ב' - ה')

Measures
Cubit (*ama* in Hebrew): approximately half a meter.

Understanding the way in which the Hebrew language uses roots to build verbs and nouns is our key to deciphering the seemingly obscure biblical description of this extraordinary building:

The Hebrew word *krutot* (כרותות), translated as "beams," is derived from the root *karot* (כרת) meaning to cut down a tree or a branch (or to amputate a limb). Therefore, we may assume that these "beams" were actually ramified cedar branches still covevered with needles. These branches could be bracketed horizontally into the cedar pillars and together **simulate live cedars**. (Such a construction could even use the top branches as supports for the "beams that were upon the...pillars.") Now what remains to clarify is how these "trees" turned into a "forest." The verb *hashkef* (השקף) meaning to see through, and the adjective *shakuf* (שקוף) meaning transparent, derive from the root *shakof* (שקף). The verb *khazo* (חזה) meaning to see, and the noun *khozeh* (חוזה) meaning prophet (one who has the power to **see** the future), derives from the root *khazo*. The "window frames in three rows" of the *Revised Standard Version* (or the "beams" of the *Jewish Publication Society*) are intended as translations for "three rows of *shkufim*" in the Hebrew original. If we understand these *shkufim* as "transparent," we see that each "transparent row" was just a passage between two rows of the above mentioned "trees." From this it is quite clear that the Hebrew text is correct in describing **four** (not three) rows of pillars, and between them **three** "transparet" rows, meaning "see-through" passages. The "window" (which was "opposite window in three tiers") in the *Revised Standard Version*, or the "light" (which

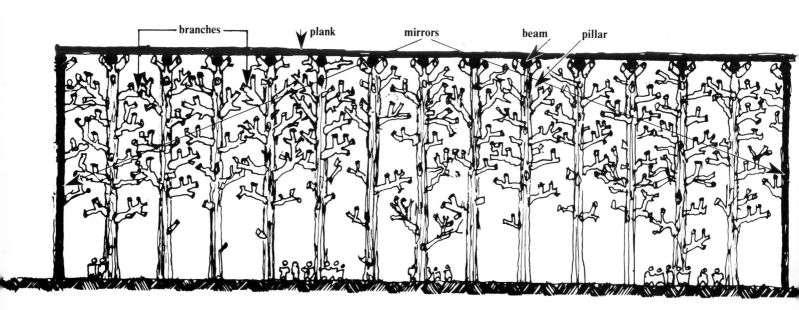

"was over against light in three ranks") in the *Jewish Publication Society* version, are translations of the word *mekheza* (מחזה) in the Hebrew text. We believe that this unique Hebrew word, which does not appear anywhere else in the Bible (and therefore remained obscure), may be rendered simply as **mirror**, stemming from the root *khazo* (to see), just as the common Hebrew word for mirror, *mar'a* (מראה), is derived from the root *rao* (ראה) also meaning to see. **The use of facing mirrors at both ends of each one of the "see-through passages" gave the visitor the illusion of being in a literally infinite forest - the "trees" reflected endlessly in the opposing mirrors - the "House of the Forest of Lebanon."**

Based on the above, we suggest a new interpretive English translation:

"He built the House of the Forest of Lebanon, a hundred cubits long, fifty cubits broad, and thirty cubits high, constructed of four rows of cedar pillars into which branches of cedar were bracketed. And it was roofed with forty-five cedar planks, fifteen in a row which were laid upon the beams that rested upon the pillars. And there were three see-through (transparent) passages, and mirror adjacent to mirror three times. And all the openings and doorframes were transparent squares, and on the opposite side too there was mirror adjacent to mirror three times."

(I Kings 7:2-5)

"King Solomon made two hundred shields of beaten gold, and six hundred (shekels of) gold went to the making of

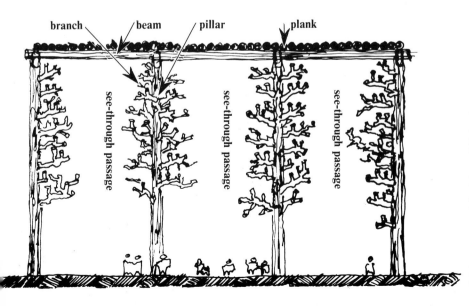

branch / beam / pillar / plank

see-through passage | see-through passage | see-through passage

Weights
Shekel and *mina*: According to the *Encyclopaedia Judaica*, v.16, p.385, the *shekel* may be equivalent to 11.3 grams, and the *mina* to fifty shekels. Therefore each shield weighed 6,780 grams (or over six and a half kilograms of gold!) and each buckler, 1,695 grams of gold.

The House of the Forest of Lebanon - cross section

p. 102

The House of the Forest of Lebanon - profile

Plans specially drawn for Neot Kedumim by the architect M. Ben-Horin.

103

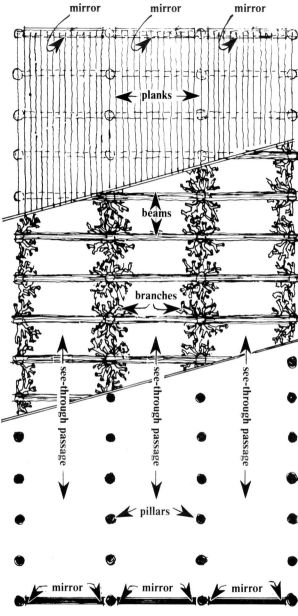

mirror   mirror   mirror

← planks →

beams

branches

see-through passage see-through passage see-through passage

← pillars →

mirror mirror mirror

The House of the Forest of Lebanon - plan showing three levels

p. 105

The snow-white flowers of the hyssop
"Cleanse me with hyssop that I may be pure, wash me that I may become whiter than snow."

each one; he also made three hundred bucklers of beaten gold, and three *minas* of gold went to the making of each buckler... The king put these into the House of the Forest of Lebanon."

(I Kings 10:16-17)

Clearly the House of the Forest of Lebanon was most carefully planned to astound the diplomatic and trade delegations that came to Solomon from far and wide, as well as to leave an indelible impression of the glory, glamour, and wealth of Jerusalem.

The attitude of the Bible to this ostentation was ambivalent. Alongside the national pride obvious in the descriptions of the splendor of Solomon's kingdom, there is an element of sharp criticism:

"And Solomon got together many chariots and horses; he had one thousand four hundred chariots and twelve thousand horses, and he stabled some in the chariot-towns and kept others at hand in Jerusalem. The king made silver as common in Jerusalem as stones, and cedar as plentiful as sycomore in the lowlands. Horses were imported from Egypt... Chariots were imported from Egypt for six hundred (pieces of) silver each, and horses for one hundred and fifty... And King Solomon was a lover of women and besides Pharaoh's daughter he married many foreign women: Moabite, Ammonite, Edomite, Sidonian and Hittite from the nations with whom the Lord had forbidden the Israelites to intermarry."

(I Kings 10:26-11:2)

These descriptions are especially cutting in light of the strict warning in the book of Deuteronomy:

"You shall choose as king the man whom the Lord your God has chosen. He must be one of your own people... He is not to acquire large numbers of horses, for he shall not send people back to Egypt for the sake of having many horses... He is not to have many wives and so be led astray; nor is he to acquire great quantities of silver and gold for himself... **that he shall not become proud above his people**...and turn away from these commandments."

(Deuteronomy 17:15-20)

"Shall you rule because you preen yourself with cedars?"

Pride is symbolized by the **cedar** in Jewish tradition:

"This shall be the law of the leper on the day of his cleansing... The priest shall command for him...cedar wood... and ...hyssop."

(Leviticus 14:2-4)

"Said Rabbi Isaac bar Tavlai [44]: What is the significance of cedar wood and hyssop...for the leper? They say to him: You were proud like the cedar and the Holy One, Blessed be He, humbled you like this hyssop that is crushed by everyone."

(Midrash Hagadol, Metzora 14)

One of the best known lepers in the Bible was the great king Uzziah, who ruled the kingdom of Judah some 200 years after Solomon:

"His fame spread far and wide, for he was so wonderfully gifted that he became very powerful. But when he grew powerful his pride led to his own undoing... And leprosy broke out on his forehead in the presence of the priests...and they hurried him out of the Temple, and indeed he himself hastened to leave, because the Lord had smitten him. And King Uzziah remained a leper till the day of his death...while his son Jotham was comptroller of the household and regent. The other events of Uzziah's reign, from the first to last, are recorded by the prophet Isaiah."

(II Chronicles 26:15-22)

According to historians, this period was the height of political and

Hyssop: moss or shrub?

For many years, especially in European countries, it was accepted that the biblical *ezov* was moss or lichen, that short, clumpy plant growing on tree trunks, rocks, and walls, frequently on the shaded, moist northern exposure. Rashi [60] objects to this identification (in his commentary on Exodus 12:22), saying: "*Ezov* is a plant that has branches." Many places in the writings of the Sages indicate that *ezov* has branches. For instance: "The *ezov*...was dipped with its stem and its branches..." (Tosefta Para 12,3). It is impossible, therefore, for the hyssop to be moss or lichen, which does not have visible branches and of which it certainly cannot be said that it could be "dipped with its stem and its branches."

Then, too, there is the saying: "If a flame catches the cedars, what will the hyssop do that is in the rock?" Despite its biblical sounding language, this comes from the Gemara (Mo'ed Katan 25b), from the eulogy recited by the famed orator Bar-Kipok over Rav Ashi [59]. This saying gives us additional proof that the hyssop is "a kind of tree" whose branches easily catch fire. If the hyssop were really moss growing on rock faces, this saying could never have been composed. For what danger is there for the moist, spongy moss, growing in damp places, even when the mighty cedars of Lebanon catch fire?

Ibn Ezra [61] in his commentary on this same passage (Exodus 12:22) says: "The Gaon identified hyssop with the Arabic *za'tar*, *oregano* in the foreign language, which is one of the most important spice plants. It is not possible that the Gaon is right because the Bible says that 'the hyssop grows in the rock' and therefore I do not know what it is. However it seems that it cannot be a large plant because it is the opposite of the cedar mentioned in the verse." It seems that Ibn Ezra was not familiar with the hyssop's various habitats, one of which is rock outcroppings (as can be seen in all the hilly regions of Israel). Therefore he did not accept the Gaon's identification.

Because the *ezov* is a plant with a woody stem and branches, it is listed among the **trees** of which Solomon spoke: "He discoursed of the **trees**, from the cedar of Lebanon to the hyssop that grows in the rock." (I Kings 5:13) Solomon spoke of trees, from the mightiest to the lowliest, from the haughtiest to the most humble.

---

p. 106

right
The hyssop flourishes even in the arid mountains of Sinai.

left, top to bottom
"Ezov is a plant that has branches" (Rashi) and not moss or lichen which do not have branches.

military power of the kingdom of Judah and a time of economic flowering. It is described by Isaiah:

"The land is filled with silver and gold,
and there is no end to their treasure;
their land is filled with horses,
and there is no end to their chariots;
their land is filled with idols,
and they bow down to the work of their own hands,
to what their fingers have made."

(Isaiah 2:7-8)

Just as the book of Kings speaks of Solomon's transgressions against the three things forbidden a king of Israel (numerous horses, pagan wives, gold and silver), so Isaiah too speaks out against these same transgressions committed by King Uzziah, who had become too proud. The punishment is not long in coming:

"For the Lord of Hosts has a day of doom waiting
for each that is proud and arrogant,
for each that is high - so that it is brought low,
for all the cedars of Lebanon, lofty and high,
and for all the oaks of Bashan...
Then man's pride shall be brought low,
and the loftiness of man shall be humbled
and the Lord alone shall be exalted on that day."

(Isaiah 2:12-17)

It is reasonable to assume that the description "all the cedars of Lebanon, lofty and high" does not refer only to the actual cedars glamorizing Jerusalem but also, together with the oaks of Bashan, to "man's pride that shall be brought low and the loftiness of man which shall be humbled." Isaiah broadly hints at Uzziah's sin of pride for which he was struck with leprosy. It is as though the Lord is saying to the proud person: You want to set yourself apart from your fellows? I will help you! You will be struck with leprosy and cast out from the community of man. When the cured leper asks to rejoin society, he must commit himself never again to become proud like the cedar but rather to be humble like the hyssop.

The hyssop (*Majorana syriaca* (L.) Rafin. or *Origanum syriacum* (L.) Sieb.) is a grayish shrub with thin woody branches; neither its leaves nor its flowers are outstanding in any way. It makes do with very little, sometimes even growing out of the smallest cracks in stone ("in the rock"), yet is highly valued for its fragrance and flavor. The hyssop is an important spice and medicinal plant, while its dry branches are excellent kindling. The best known food made from the hyssop in the Middle East is a powder known by its Arabic name, *za'tar*. It is a mixture of crushed or powdered hyssop leaves, sesame seeds, ground sumac fruit, salt, and pepper. The words of Rabbi bar Tavlai [44], "the hyssop is crushed by all," reflect its widespread use for spice,

A safe sumac
The sumac used in *za'tar* is *Rhus coriaria* L. and not the highly poisonous sumac, *Rhus* (or *Toxicodendron) vernix*, which does not grow in the Middle East.

p. 109

"And not any other hyssop that has a descriptive name."
According to the identifications of Ephraim Hareuveni:
right, top and bottom
The "date palm" hyssop (or "tea" hyssop), Micromeria fruticosa *(L.) Druce.*
center
Roman hyssop, Satureja thymbra
left, top and bottom
Ezovion, Teucrium polium *L.*

p. 110

Ezov kokhli, Lavandula stoechas *L.*

108

fragrance, and medicine. Yet the lowly hyssop never becomes proud because of its numerous useful qualities, but remains humble in appearance and modest in its demands.

This symbolism of the hyssop versus the cedar also helps us to understand the entreaty of King David after the prophet Nathan rebukes him for his deeds with Bathsheba: "Cleanse me with hyssop that I may be pure; wash me that I may become whiter than snow." (Psalm 51:9) By taking Bathsheba as he did, David arrogantly accorded himself the unjust privileges assumed by foreign kings, thus "he became proud above his people." Therefore, David's prayer for forgiveness can be understood like the plea of the leper: I was proud and haughty like the cedar, and now I beseech You to make me humble like this hyssop with which I ask to be cleansed.

Biblical tradition condemns overdone majesty and glamour. Self-aggrandizement and adornment with cedar was frowned upon. However, in King Solomon's time this opposition was overshadowed by the comfort and plenty enjoyed by wide circles in Solomon's great, rich kingdom that was at peace with all the nations. As evidenced by the attitude of the author of the biblical narration, in that period the flaunting of cedars, gold, silver, and horses was understood as necessary for the development of the wide-ranging trade which materialized under Solomon. The various ambassadors must have been greatly impressed by the wealth and might of Solomon's kingdom. But this was not the view taken by Isaiah towards the end of King Uzziah's reign.

About 150 years after Uzziah - and some 350 years after Solomon - the prophet Jeremiah too condemned the importing of cedars and their arrogant use. The kingdom of Judah was then a beaten and weak nation that existed as a vassal of Egypt until later conquest by Babylon. The involvement of Jehoiakim, King of Judah, with superfluous building outraged Jeremiah:

> "Shame on the man who builds his house by unjust means and completes its roof chamber by fraud, making his countrymen work without payment, giving them no wage for their labor. Shame on the man who says, 'I will build a spacious house with airy roof-chambers, set windows in it, **panel it with cedar** and paint it with vermilion!' **Shall you rule because you preen yourself with cedars?** Therefore these are the words of the Lord concerning Jehoiakim, son of Josiah, king of Judah: For him no mourner... He shall have a donkey's burial, dragged along and flung out beyond the gates of Jerusalem!'" (Jeremiah 22:13-19)

"For these are the words of the Lord about the royal house of Judah: Though you are Gilead to me, **the heights of Lebanon,** I swear that I will make you a wilderness, a land of unpeopled cities. I will dedicate an armed host to fight

The terebinth and the oak: glory and collapse, destruction and hope

"I asked, 'How long, my Lord?' And He replied:
'Until cities fall in ruins and are deserted,
and houses are left without people,
and the country lies waste and desolate,
For the Lord will banish the population
and the desolation shall spread through the land.
And even if a tenth part yet remains in it,
it too shall be consumed,
like the terebinth and the oak in their fall (season),
their (dormant) trunk remains carrying the holy seed within." (Isaiah 6:11-13)

As the Bible tells us, these words were spoken "in the year King Uzziah died." (Isaiah 6:1) Whether this is the year in which King Uzziah was struck with leprosy and was "relieved of all duties and excluded from the house of the Lord, while his son Jotham was comptroller of the household and regent" (II Chronicles 26:21), or whether this was the year of Uzziah's actual death when he "was succeeded by his son Jotham" (II Chronicles 26:23), it is clear that this latter half of the eighth century BCE was a period of political and military glory in the kingdom of Judah. During the reign of Uzziah, the borders of Judah extended to those which had existed under King Solomon two centuries earlier and included Eilat, all the land of the Edomites, and the Philistine territories on the coastal plain. Jotham continued the projects of his father, Uzziah, fortifying the desert frontier, defeating the Ammonites, and extending his sphere of influence to areas that had been part of the kingdom of Israel in the days of Jeroboam ben Jehoash in the first half of the eighth century BCE. But together with increasing military, political, and economic strength, class differences grew in Judah, and oppression and exploitation of the people increased.

Isaiah fought against these injustices and censured the hypocrisy of offering sacrifices in the Temple while the laws of the Bible were publicly violated. He predicted that this moral degeneration would bring the collapse of the kingdom's power and lead to conquest by foreign armies. But it was not easy to prove this danger to a people certain of strength and wealth. In the verses cited, Isaiah found a simile that was forceful because it describes familiar and undisputed phenomena. To understand the simile it is necessary to learn about the special autumnal characteristics of the terebinth and the oak.

With the beginning of the rainy season in Israel, the terebinth *(Pistacia palaestina)* becomes conspicuous among all the green forest trees. In November-December the terebinth's leaves turn from green to variegated reds and yellows. The special beauty and glory of the terebinth at this time surpasses that of all other forest trees in Israel. This is the glory to which Isaiah compares the kingdom of Judah in the period in which he prophesies. True, Judah, at the height of its majesty, persuades itself that it is superior to the kingdom of Israel and the surrounding nations - as the terebinth is preeminent in the forest at this season. But the terebinth's breathtaking glory is but a symptom of the seasonal death of each and every leaf. Not many days will pass and the resplendent leaves will drop, leaving the tree naked. This is the picture Isaiah presents to his audience: Although now Judah stands at the peak of success, each cell of its social structure is dying, though this is not yet visible to the undiscerning eye. Just a little longer and all the glory will fade away.

But together with the autumnal terebinth, Isaiah presents his listeners with the oak in its fall season. Familiarity with the oak reveals that Isaiah did not pair these two trees for mere "poetic" effect, but because the oak and the terebinth together have yet another figurative meaning. Destiny beyond the immediate future is hinted at - developments after destruction.

Unlike the terebinth, the Tabor oak *(Quercus ithaburensis)* does not turn color before its leaves drop in winter. The oak is distinguished for another characteristic: After its leaves drop, its branches stay bare for only a short time. Within two to three weeks new buds begin to burst forth in a fresh, light green. Newly opening buds sprout from the axils of the dry leaves that have not yet dropped from the oak. At the same time one can see on the ground newly sprouting acorns, the one-seed fruits of the oak that ripen the previous summer and drop to the ground with the start of the rainy season. A new generation of oaks begins.

Thus Isaiah shows the destruction with which the Lord shall punish the kingdom of Judah as

Cedar giants in the mountains of Lebanon
Hannah Hareuveni is the tiny figure to the left of the cedar. (Photographed by the author in 1936.)

112

against you, a ravening horde, **they shall cut down your choicest cedars** and fling them on the fire."

(Jeremiah 22:6-7)

Of **Jerusalem**, Jeremiah says:

> **"You who dwell in Lebanon, who make your nests among the cedars,** how you will groan when the pains come upon you, like the pangs of a woman in labor! As surely as I am the Living God, you, Koniah (Jehoiakhin), son of Jehoiakim, king of Judah, shall no longer be the signet ring on My right hand. I will pull you off. I will hand you over to those who seek your life, to those you fear, to Nebuchadnezzar of Babylon and to the Chaldaeans!"   (Jeremiah 22:23-25)

Similar warnings, both in style and content, are heard from the prophet Habakkuk. Although Jehoiakim is not directly mentioned, it seems that the words are addressed to him, as were the words of Jeremiah:

> "Woe betide him who seeks unjust gain for his house, to build his nest on a height, to escape disaster!... Woe betide him who has built a town with bloodshed and founded a city on fraud...**The wrong of Lebanon shall sweep over you,**... because of the bloodshed and violence done in the land, to the city and its inhabitants."   (Habakkuk 2:9-17)

"The wrong of Lebanon" has been interpreted by many as referring to the king of Babylon, on the assumption that the Babylonian army destroyed cedars of Lebanon for the purpose of war. Habakkuk says: "I am raising up the Chaldaeans, that savage and impetuous nation, who cross the wide tracts of the earth to take possession of homes not theirs." (Habakkuk 1:6) But in the continuation of the passage it becomes clear that Habakkuk is addressing himself here not to Babylon, but to Jehoiakim - the same Jehoiakim who was crowned thanks to the patronage of Egypt and later surrendered to the king of Babylon, then within three years rebelled against him. Jehoiakim boasted of ruling Jerusalem through oppression and violence, all the while building superfluous and glamorous buildings with cedars of Lebanon. In our opinion, **these actions of Jehoiakim are the ones labeled by Habakkuk "the wrong of Lebanon"** - the wrong committed by the **king of Jerusalem**. And the Lord's judgment will be turned against Jehoiakim with the coming of the Chaldaeans.

Ezekiel, the prophet who left Jerusalem to go into exile with Jehoiakim's son, Jehoiakhin (called Koniah by Jeremiah), also refers to **Jerusalem** by the name **"Lebanon"** and calls **Jehoiakhin "the very top of the cedar."**:

but a transition at whose end shall arise a new generation bearing hope of the future. The destruction is not total; just as the bare, leafless trunk carries within it the vital force of the young buds shortly to begin their new life, so Judah carries "the holy seed within."

The period of Judah's grandeur and glory is the repository also of its approaching collapse. Conversely, the impending destruction carries within it the seeds of a new society built on the moral precepts that are the "holy seed" of the Bible.

(see pictures on pp. 123-124)

The willow of Babylon vs. the grapevine of Judah

Ezekiel's "parable-riddle" in chapter 17 is one of the most interesting parables in the Bible. Its real meaning is illuminated when one is familiar with the specified trees and with their native growing regions. The historical background is equally important.

In the beginning of the sixth century BCE, Nebuchadnezzar, the great king of Babylon, attacked Judah and its capital, Jerusalem, taking captive to Babylon King Jehoiakhin, his court, wise men (including Ezekiel), army and commanders. Nebuchadnezzar also set up Jehoiakhin's uncle, Zedekiah, to rule in Judah as a vassal king. Instead of living quietly on Babylon's bounty, Zedekiah rebelled and called on the pharaoh of Egypt to free him from Babylon's yoke. As prophesied both by Ezekiel and Jeremiah, Nebuchadnezzar was enraged at this betrayal by Zedekiah, with whom he had a sworn covenant. Nebuchadnezzar sent his armies back to Judah and destroyed Jerusalem and Solomon's Temple in 586 BCE.

The dramatic events leading to the fateful destruction are vividly described by Ezekiel. He catches the attention of his audience by "propounding a riddle and relating a parable," (Ezekiel 17:2) for the events he describes take place **before** Babylon's vengeance for Judah's betrayal:

> "The great eagle with the great wings and the long pinions, with full plumage and brilliant colors, came to the Lebanon and seized the top of the cedar. He plucked off its topmost boughs and carried them off to the land of the traders and set them in a city of merchants."

> (Ezekiel 17:3-4)

As Ezekiel himself explains in verse 12-13, the great eagle is Nebuchadnezzar, who came to Jerusalem (Lebanon, as Jerusalem was frequently called), where he seized Jehoiakhin, who was the top of the cedar, and "his mother, his courtiers, commanders, and officers...as well as all the craftsmen and smiths; only the poorest people in the land were left" (II Kings 24:12,14). Nebuchadnezzar took the captives to Babylon, "the land of the traders" and set them down there in "the city of merchants."

The continuation of the riddle-parable can be understood only by correcting an existing misconception in translations that the Hebrew word *kakh* in this verse (17:5) is a verb rather than a

Thistle (hoah, Scolymus maculatus) **in a wheat field.**

"**The great eagle** with broad wings and long pinions, in full plumage, richly patterned, **came to Lebanon and took the very top of the cedar tree**... Say to the rebellious people, do you not know what this means? **The king of Babylon came to Jerusalem and took its king and its ministers...**"

(Ezekiel 17:3,11)

Self-aggrandizement by the use of cedars was not solely the characteristic of the kings of Judah. For a time, the rulers of the kingdom of Israel were also enamored of the glamor symbolized by the cedar, as is apparent from the story of Jehoash, king of Israel, and of Amaziah (Uzziah's father), king of Judah:

> "Then Amaziah sent messengers to Jehoash...king of Israel, to meet in battle. But Jehoash king of Israel sent this answer to Amaziah king of Judah: **'The thistle** *(hoah)* **in Lebanon** sent to **the cedar in Lebanon** saying, 'Give your daughter in marriage to my son.' But a wild beast in Lebanon, passing by, trampled the thistle. You have defeated Edom, and you have become arrogant. Keep your glory and stay at home. Why should you involve yourself in disaster and destroy yourself, and Judah with you?'"
>
> (II Kings 14:8-10)

Thus Jehoash, king of Israel, mocks Amaziah, king of Judah. Although Amaziah rules in **Jerusalem (called by him, as by previous generations, "Lebanon")**, in the eyes of Jehoash, Amaziah is nothing but "the thistle in Lebanon" - not "the cedar in Lebanon" he fancies himself. On the other hand, Jehoash sees himself as a cedar of Lebanon who is asked by the thistle in Lebanon to marry into his august family. Jehoash hints to Amaziah that in times past there was indeed marriage between the families of the king of Judah and the king of Israel, but that was a period when **both** were powerful and majestic "cedars of Lebanon": "When Jehoshaphat (king of Judah, Amaziah's great-great-grandfather) had become very wealthy and renowned, he allied himself by marriage with Ahab (king of Israel)." (II Chronicles 18:1) Just as Jehoshaphat "became ever more powerful" (II Chronicles 17:12), so too Ahab, who smote Aram (Syria), strengthened his ties with Tyre and rose on the tide of economic prosperity to build fortifications and magnificent buildings, including the "Ivory House" (I Kings 22:39) in the Sidonian tradition.

Jehoash's pride in the cedars of Lebanon had some legitimacy in the past history of the kingdom of Israel and its treaty with Tyre in the days of Omri and Omri's son, Ahab. Some fifty years after the war between Amaziah and Jehoash, and more than one hundred years after the death of Ahab, there is still an echo of this boasting with cedars on the part of the kings of Israel (whose capital was Samaria). In the words of Isaiah:

> "All the people shall know,
> Ephraim and the dwellers in Samaria,
> (Who say) in their pride and arrogance,
> The bricks are fallen, but we will build in hewn stone;
> The sycomores are hacked down,
> But we will use cedars instead.!"
>
> (Isaiah 9:8-9)

plant name. As identified by Rabbi Abahu in the Gemara (Sukka 34a), the *kakh* is, in fact, the willow *(Salix sp.)*. In the continuation of the verse, Ezekiel mentions the *tzaftzafa*, which was mistranslated by many as willow instead of poplar *(Populus sp.)*. The real meaning can be understood only if we know that there is a tree growing on the banks of the Euphrates River which has characteristics of **both** the willow and the poplar. This is a tree called *Populus euphratica*, a member of the *Salix* (willow) family. Therefore, it is logical to understand these two names in Ezekiel, *kakh* and *tzaftzafa*, as the combination name for the one tree - the "willow-poplar" - native to Babylon. The following translation of verse 5 is a result of this clarification:

> "He (Nebuchadnezzar) then took from the seed of the land and planted it in a fertile field; he planted and set it like a willow-poplar *(kakh-tzaftzafa)* beside abundant water. It grew and became a spreading vine of low stature. (He had intended) that its twigs should turn to him, and that its roots should stay under him; (but) it became a vine, produced branches, and sent out boughs."
>
> (Ezekiel 17:5-6)

Nebuchadnezzar planted a local seed, Zedekiah, in the fertile soil of Judah, intending for it to grow into a tree native to Babylon - the willow-poplar *(kakh-tzaftzafa)*. But instead of becoming an obedient vassal (the native willow-poplar as Nebuchadnezzar had intended), Zedekiah grew into a grapevine, the symbol of Judah, and sent out his boughs in another direction.

> "But there was another great eagle with great wings and full plumage; and this vine now bent its roots in his direction and sent out its twigs toward him, that he might water it more than the bed where it was planted, though it was planted in rich soil beside abundant water, so that it might grow branches and produce boughs and be a noble vine."
>
> (Ezekiel 17:7-8)

This other great eagle was Egypt, probably Pharaoh Hophra, with whom Zedekiah planned an alliance against Babylon. It was towards this second eagle that the vine of Judah sent out its boughs, seeking better conditions even though, for a vassal state, conditions in Judah under Nebuchadnezzar were good and peaceful ("it was planted in rich soil beside abundant water").

Ezekiel then leaves the language of riddle and parable and says point blank that a pact with Pharaoh will not avail Zedekiah. Babylon will sweep down once again, this time scattering the remnants of Judah in every direction, and taking

Zedekiah captive back to Babylon. Indeed we know from II Kings 25 how bitter the end really was: Nebuchadnezzar "slaughtered Zedekiah's sons before his eyes; then Zedekiah's eyes were put out. He was chained in bronze fetters and brought to Babylon." Thus was the downfall of Judah, of Jerusalem, and of the Holy Temple.

The southern wind is the hardest of all

There are winter days in Israel when the southern wind (primarily the southwesterly wind) brings rain clouds and abundant rain to the land, "like showers on young growth" (Deuteronomy 32:2). On the other hand, between early April and late May, the southern wind (primarily the southeasterly wind) can bring very high temperatures and excessive dryness. (See *Nature in Our Biblical Heritage*, pp.30-42.) "The southern wind is the hardest of all (to bear)." (Baba Batra 25a) It seems that this description of the southern wind - the only one that can so dry out a full-grown cedar tree that it is possible to uproot and overturn it - applies only to the special conditions in which **cedars were planted in Jerusalem**. This is in sharp contrast to the native habitat of the cedars in the mountains of Lebanon, where snow and rain are plentiful, while the influence of the hot (southern) desert wind is relatively mild. Jerusalem, quite the reverse, is exposed to these southern winds with telling effect, and receives nowhere near the precipitation available in Lebanon's mountains.

The negative stance in Jewish tradition toward the cedar is also reflected in the following:

"Rabbi Samuel bar Nahmani [40] said in the name of Rabbi Jonathan [33]: What is the meaning of the verse, 'The blows a friend gives are well meant, but the kisses of an enemy are perfidious'? (Proverbs 27:6) Better is the curse that Ahijah of Shiloh pronounced on Israel than the blessings with which Balaam the wicked blessed them. Ahijah of Shiloh cursed them by comparing them with the reed. He said to Israel: 'The Lord will strike Israel until it sways like a reed in water.' As the reed grows by the water, its stock grows new shoots (if the stock is cut it grows again). Its roots are many, and even though all the winds of the universe come and blow at it, they cannot move it from its place, for it sways with the winds; as soon as they (the winds) have dropped, the reed resumes its upright position. But Balaam the wicked blessed them by comparing them with the cedar, as it is said, 'As cedars beside the waters.' The cedar does not grow by the waterside; its stock does not grow new shoots (if it is cut down). Its roots are not many, and even though all the winds of the universe blow at it they cannot move it from its place; if, however, the southern wind blows at it, it uproots it and turns it upside down. Moreover, the reed merited that a pen be made of it for the writing of the Bible. Our Rabbis have taught: A man should always be flexible as the reed and never stiff as the cedar." (Ta'anit 20a)

116

A clump of reeds
"Even though all the winds of the universe...blow at it,
they cannot move it from its place, for it sways with the winds."

Kings and Prophets

United Kingdom

SAUL	1020-1000 BCE
DAVID	1000-965
SOLOMON	965-927

Divided Kingdoms

Israel

Jeroboam I	927-907	*AHIJAH*
Nadab	907-906	
Baasha	906-883	
Elah	883-882	
Zimri	882	
OMRI	882-871	
AHAB	871-852	*ELIJAH*
Ahaziah	852-851	
Joram	851-845	
Jehu	845-818	
Jehoahaz	818-802	
JEHOASH	802-787	
JEROBOAM II	787-747	
Zechariah	747	
Shallum	747	
Menahem	747-738	
Pekahiah	737-736	
Pekah	735-732	
Hoshea	731-723	

Judah

Rehoboam	926-910	
Abijah	910-908	
Asa	908-868	
JEHOSHAPHAT	868-847	
Jehoram	847-845	
Ahaziah	845	
Athaliah	845-840	
Joash	840-801	
AMAZIAH	801-773	
UZZIAH	773-736	*AMOS*
JOTHAM	756-741	*ISAIAH*
AHAZ	741-725	
HEZEKIAH	725-697	
Manasseh	696-642	
Amon	641-640	
JOSIAH	639-609	*JEREMIAH*
Jehoahaz	609	
JEHOIAKIM	608-598	
JEHOIAKHIN (KONIAH)	598	*EZEKIEL*
ZEDEKIAH	597-587	

Names in capital letters indicate
names mentioned in this book.
All dates are approximate.

From where acacia for the Tabernacle?

Different species of acacia stand out in the landscapes of the Negev and Sinai. The Bible tells us that the bars and planks for the Tabernacle, as well as the ark, the table, the altar, and the incense altar were made from this tree. (See Exodus 25-26 and 36-37.) Although most acacia trees known today in Sinai do not develop straight, tall trunks, it is possible to see individual acacia trees (see picture on p. 119) whose trunk is straight and tall enough even for use as the central bar of the Tabernacle which was about fifteen meters long. (See Exodus 36:21-33.) From what is told in Exodus 25:5 and 35:24, the acacia wood was brought by the Children of Israel during their wandering in the Sinai Wilderness as an offering for the building of the Tabernacle, together with other appropriate contributions:

"Men and women alike came and freely brought clasps, earrings, rings, and pendants, gold ornaments of every kind, every one of them presenting a special gift of gold to the Lord. And everyone brought what he possessed of violet, purple, and scarlet stuff, fine linen and goats' hair, tanned rams' skins and porpoise hides. Everyone, setting aside a contribution of silver or copper, brought it as a contribution to the Lord, and **all who had in their possession acacia wood suitable for any part of the work brought it.**'

(Exodus 35:22-24)

The importance of each acacia tree in this area is well known. It provides important sustenance for animals, as well as shade for people and their possessions. It seems to us, therefore, that the Bible is stressing the fact that the Israelites had acacia lumber on hand in their tents for use; from that supply they contributed wood for the building of the Tabernacle and its artifacts. This obviated the need for chopping down additional trees. Compilers of the midrashim went even further, seeing in the phrase "all who had in their possession" a clue that the source of this contributed acacia wood was not Sinai at all.

"From where were the planks for the Tabernacle? The patriarch Jacob planted them when he went down to Egypt. He said to his sons: 'Children, you will be redeemed from here, and the Holy One, Blesed be He, will say to you: Now that you have been redeemed, build Me a Tabernacle. So go and plant cedars. When the hour comes that you are called upon to build the Tabernacle, the cedars will be at hand.' They did exactly what their father told them - arose and planted cedars...and when the Holy One, Blessed be He, said (to Moses) to build the Tabernacle, what did He say to him? 'You shall make **the** planks for the Tabernacle - the same planks that their father (Jacob) prepared for them.' Said Rabbi Samuel bar Nahmani [40]: 'There were twenty-four varieties of cedars, and of these only seven were chosen, as it is written: 'I will plant cedars in the desert, acacia and myrtle and the oil tree, I will set in the wilderness juniper, maple, and cypress together'...and of all these only the acacia was chosen, as it is written, 'acacia wood.'"

(Tanhuma Truma 9)

As described on pp.121-122, included in the "types of cedars" with which it is permitted to perform the ceremony of the purification of the leper were those trees that the Bible saw as bestowing "the glory of Lebanon" on the desert and wilderness. According to the Sages, the Holy Temple was also called "Lebanon."(see p. 121) In this midrash we see clearly the transposition from the Holy Temple in Jerusalem, which was overlaid with cedar wood, to the Tabernacle in the wilderness, whose frame was built of acacia wood, as though saying that since the Temple was of cedar, so the Tabernacle was of "cedar." But it is written specifically "acacia"! No problem, for we have already learned from the ceremony of the purification of the leper that the acacia was "a kind of cedar." Specifically though, of all these varieties of "cedars," only the acacia was chosen for the building of the Tabernacle.

In its search for the source of the wood for the Taberacle, another midrash goes even further back to those trees that Abraham planted in Beersheva, ignoring the fact that the Bible states that Abraham planted tamarisks and not cedars:

"'So Israel (Jacob) set out with all that was his.' (Genesis 46:1) They went and cut down cedars that the Patriarch Abraham had planted in Beersheba. As it is written, 'Abraham planted tamarisks in Beersheva.' And what was their length? Thirty cubits. They had it (the wood) until the building of the Tabernacle. As it is written 'all who had in their possession **acacia** wood.' The Bible does not say there **was** acacia wood but that the people **possessed it from the beginning** (meaning from before the entry into Sinai). Said Rabbi Levi bar Haya [51]: 'In Migdal Tzabaya they were cut down and brought with them (with the Children of Israel) to Egypt, and they had neither knot nor knob.' [In other words, they were straight and smooth enough to fit through the "golden rings".] There were acacia trees in Migdal Tzabaya and they were sanctified (prohibited for use) because of the holiness of the Ark. They (the contemporary residents of the town) came and asked of Rav Hananiah [46] (about the sanctification ban) and he replied: 'Do not change the traditions of your forefathers.'"

(Shir Hashirim Raba 1,12; the story of the acacia trees from Migdal Tzabaya that were prohibited for use because of their sanctification to God, is also told in other sources.)

The name Migdal Tzabaya was given at various times to the town of Migdal on the northwestern shore of the Sea of Galilee (Migdal Nunia) and also to the Migdal near the Arab village Mukheiba in the area of Hamat Gader at the southern tip of the Sea of Galilee. (See Klein, Shmuel, *The Land of Galilee*, Mosad HaRav Kook, 1946, pp.209-211.) In this region we find the acacia species, *Acacia alba*, which does not grow in Sinai and according to botanists never grew there. Nevertheless, there was a tradition in Migdal Tzabaya which sanctified the local acacia trees because the Ark was made of acacia wood.

---

p. 119

Acacia trees in the wilderness
There are acacia tall enough to have provided the central bar of the Tabernacle.

The greening
of the wilderness

In Jewish tradition there is also a positive view of Lebanon and its cedars. The abundance of rain and snow in Lebanon, the numerous rivers flowing in their beds, the moisture retained throughout the summer, and the tall shady trees that grow there - for many generations in Jewish tradition all these were "an example in this world" of what will be in the land of Israel when the Messiah comes, both a hope and a prayer for the "greening of the wilderness."

> "I will be as dew to Israel that he may flower like a lily, strike **roots like Lebanon**, put out fresh shoots, that he may be as fair as the olive, and **fragrant as Lebanon**. Israel shall again dwell in His shade and grow grain in abundance; they shall flourish like a grapevine and be celebrated as the **wine of Lebanon**." (Hosea 14:6-8)

> "Said Rabbi Johanan [37]: The world was not worthy to enjoy the use of cedars. Why then were cedars created? For the sake of the Temple, as it is written, 'The trees of the Lord drink their fill, the cedars of Lebanon that He planted.' (Psalm 104:16) For Lebanon is the Holy Temple as is written, 'that good mountain, and the Lebanon.' (Deuteronomy 3:25)" (Breshit Raba 15,1)

> "That good mountain - this is Jerusalem. The Lebanon - this is the Holy Temple." (Midrash Hagadol, portion Va'etkhanan 3,25)

The desire to see the freshness and vitality of Lebanon spreading throughout Israel is proclaimed in Isaiah's paean to the salvation of Israel:

> "I will open up streams on the bare hills
> and fountains amid the valleys;
> I will turn the desert into ponds,
> The arid land into springs of water.
> I will plant cedars in the desert,
> Acacia and myrtle and the 'oil tree,'
> I will set in the wilderness juniper *(brosh)*, maple *(tidhar)*
> and cypress *(te'ashur)* together -
> That men may see and know,
> Consider and comprehend
> That the Lord's hand has done this,
> That the Holy One of Israel has created it." (Isaiah 41:18-20)

Are there really ten kinds of cedars?

In the Bible the cedar appears as the definitive representative of the mountains of Lebanon. But the literature of the Sages seemingly contradicts the identification of the cedar as the tree known as the cedar of Lebanon:

> "Said the Sages: There are ten kinds of cedars: cedar *(erez)*, acacia *(shita)*, myrtle *(hadass)*, and oil tree *(etz shemen)*, juniper *(brosh)*, maple *(tidhar)*, and cypress *(te'ashur)* - these are seven. When Rav Dimai [49] arrived (from Israel), he said: Add to these oak *(alon)*, plane *(armon)*, and *almog*." (Midrash Hagadol, Truma 25,10)

(This same list of ten kinds of cedars is given in different sources of the first generation of the *amoraim* [31] in the Babylonian Talmud [Rosh Hashana 23a, Baba Batra 80b, in the name of the School of Rav [35], and as a partial quotation in Ta'anit 25b] and in the Midrash Raba [Breshit 15,1, Shmot 35,1 from the words of Rav Samuel bar Nahmani [40] in the name of Rabbi Jonathan [33]], in the Midrash Tanhuma [Truma 9, in the name of Rav Samuel bar Nahmani] and also in the Jerusalem Talmud, without mentioning the source [Ktubot, chapter 7]).

A question is raised by this tradition of the *amoraim*, found in so many Jewish sources. What possible relationship did the Sages see between the actual cedar and other trees so different from the cedar in appearance, name, and habitat? This author believes that the key is to be found in the story of Rabbi Judah [25] (Tosefta Negaim 8,2; Jerusalem Talmud, Negaim, chapter 2, section 2) that the Safra (and later also the Midrash Hagadol and Yalkut Shimoni) offers to clarify which tree could be acceptable as "cedar" for the purification ceremony of the leper (Leviticus 14:1-5):

> "Can any tree be used? The Bible says: cedar. If a cedar, then is a leaf sufficient? Says the Bible: (cedar) tree. So what must be taken? A branch cut from the tree. Rabbi Hananiah ben Gamaliel [24] said: The branch must have (at least) a leaf. Said Rabbi Judah: It was my turn to preach on the sabbath and I followed Rabbi Tarfon [14] home. He said to me: Judah, my son, pass me my sandals. I did so. He passed his hand out the window, and picked up a stick (lying on the ledge) and gave it to me. He said to me: Judah, with this stick I purified three lepers and through it

p. 120

An example in this world of Isaiah's prophecy
In rainy winters, the Judean Desert bursts into verdant blossom.

taught seven *halakhot* [2]: that it is a juniper *(brosh)* branch (and is permitted for use in the ceremony of accepting the cured leper back into the community), that it has a leaf at its tip, that its length is (at least) one cubit and its width (at least) a quarter of the width of a bedpost...and that the purification of the leper could be performed when the Temple stood and after it was destroyed, as well as outside Jerusalem."

(Safra Metzora, chapter 1, 12-13)

It is significant that the tradition of the permissibility of using juniper *(brosh)*, not only cedar, in the ceremony of purifying the leper was passed on by Rabbi Tarfon specifically to Rabbi Judah. Rabbi Judah was noted for his strict rulings. For instance, Rabbi Judah ruled that the *sukka* (booth) on *Sukkot* - the Feast of Tabernacles (Booths) - must actually be built of the four species (date palm, willow, myrtle, and citron), and not that the four species should simply be brought into the *sukka* built of any available materials. The Sages disagreed with Rabbi Judah, saying that the ultimate effect of exaggerated strictness would be not greater exactitude but the very opposite: Too strict a ruling, one extremely difficult to execute (such as finding the four species in sufficient quantity to build an entire *sukka*), would simply cause people to throw up their hands and not build a *sukka* at all. (Sukka 36b,37a)

It is reasonable to assume that in the matter of the use of cedar wood in the leper's purification ceremony, Rabbi Judah was characteristically literal, declaring that **only** cedar wood could be used. His teacher, Rabbi Tarfon (who was of the priestly class), used the juniper branch to show Rabbi Judah that a priest may not neglect the ceremony of purification just because cedar wood is unavailable. It is not mere chance that this story emphasized that the purification ceremony could also be carried out when it was much harder to find cedar tree branches - after the destruction of the Temple and even outside Jerusalem.

It seems to us, therefore, that the trees listed at the beginning of this note under the general title "cedar" were not considered by the Sages at all as species related to the cedar in the botanical sense. They referred to these trees as "cedars" only as permissible replacements for use in the purification ceremony of the leper, because these trees were listed in the Bible together with the cedar in connection with "the glory of Lebanon." In this way, albeit roundabout, the symbolic meaning of the purification ceremony was also preserved: "Because you were proud like this cedar, you have been brought low by the Lord God like this hyssop that is crushed by all." In contrast to the aforementioned relaxation of the law on cedar wood, the strict requirement vis-a-vis the hyssop is striking.

"Hyssop, and not *ezovion* (in another version, Greek hyssop) and not blue hyssop and not Roman hyssop and not 'wild' hyssop and not any other hyssop that has a descriptive name."

(Safra Metzora, chapter 1,16; and many other places)

Unlike the cedar, which even King Solomon acquired at great effort and cost, the hyssop grows wild in many places and was even raised in home garden plots. It is to be found in every marketplace, for it is used for food, spice, medicine, and even as kindling. It was impossibile that branches of the hyssop would be difficult to find close at hand when needed. Therefore the Sages were careful to stipulate that none of the plants nicknamed "hyssop" was acceptable for use in the purification ceremony, even if a substitute was similar to the true hyssop in fragrance, taste or use. For the ceremony of the purification of the leper, only the hyssop "that is crushed by all" can be used, for its use is more widespread than that of any of the other "hyssops," none of which is mentioned in the Bible.

Another symbolic virtue of the hyssop in the purification ceremony is its **white flowers**. In many places the Sages pinned down the identity of the "scarlet stuff" *(shani)*; it must be made from the authentic snail from which the red *shani* (often translated as "crimson") is produced and not from any other source: "Be your sins like 'scarlet stuff,' they can turn snow-white; be they red as the 'crimson snail,' they can become like fleece." (Isaiah 1:18) Possibly the Sages saw in the snow-white flowers of the hyssop the same kind of symbolism, conceivably implied by the words of King David: "Cleanse me with **hyssop** that I may be pure; wash me that I may be **whiter than snow**." (Psalms 51:9) All the other plants nicknamed *"ezov"* have flowers of various shades of blue and purple (with the exception of the white-flowered *ezovion* which differs from the other "hyssops" in that it has specific medicinal use). (See Ephraim Hareuveni's article, "Types of Hyssop," *[Ezovim L'mineihem]*, "Tarbitz," vol.20-21, 1949/50 in which he identifies the various "hyssops" in detail.) Perhaps flower color is a reinforcing reason for the prohibition of these other plants in the ceremony of the purification of the leper.

The cedar and the hyssop are also essential ingredients of the "ceremony of the burning of the red heifer" from whose ashes the "cleansing water" was prepared for the purification of one who has touched a corpse (Numbers 19). This ceremony was performed only in the Holy Temple where, thanks to King Solomon's efforts, there was no problem in finding cedar wood. We believe this, therefore, is the reason that there is no hint in the Talmud or any other sources permitting the use in this ceremony of any of the aforementioned "kinds of cedar". On the contrary, the midrashim of the *tannaim* [6] teach of the scrupulous care not to burn in the fire prepared for the "red heifer" any wood except that of the cedar, nor any hyssop but the true hyssop:

"The priest shall take wood. Can he take any wood? Says the Bible: cedar (only)! And if the cedar, can he take only the leaf of the cedar? Says the Bible: cedar wood. What does the Bible mean? Wood from the heart of the cedar... And the hyssop? Not *ezovion*, not the blue hyssop and not the 'wild' hyssop and not the Roman hyssop but only the true hyssop that bears no descriptive name."

(Midrash Hagadol, Para 19,6; Sifri Hukat 124; Sifri Zuta Hukat 6)

These midrashic traditions accord with the strictness reflected in the Mishna in the description of the casting of the cedar and the hyssop into the fire on which the red heifer was burned:

"He said to the bystanders: 'Is this cedarwood? Is this cedarwood? Is this hyssop? Is this hyssop? Is this scarlet stuff *(shani)*? Is this scarlet stuff?' Three times he repeated each question and they answered him 'yea, yea!' - three times to each question." (Para 3,10)

Such emphasis on "three times to each question" appears in the Mishna only one other time, in the description of the ceremony of the *Omer* barley harvest (Menahot 10,3), and there the reason is also given. "And why all this? Because of the Boethusian faction who maintained that the reaping of the *omer* was not to take place at the conclusion of the (first day of the Passover) festival." Here, in the matter of the burning of the red heifer, where there is no hint of disagreement with the Boethusians, it seems that the emphatic concern is to insure that the priest not be misled to take any tree other than cedar, as was permitted by the relaxation of the law in the purification ceremony of the leper.

Even though Lebanon is not mentioned in Isaiah chapter 41 by name, its choice representatives - the cedar and the juniper - are present in these verses leading the two categories of trees which will glorify the desert and the wilderness when these will become areas filled with water like Lebanon.

> "The arid desert shall be glad,
> The wilderness shall rejoice
> And shall blossom like a *havatzelet* flower.
> It shall blossom abundantly,
> It shall also exult and shout.
> It shall receive the glory of Lebanon,
> The splendor of Carmel and Sharon.
> They shall behold the glory of the Lord,
> The splendor of our God."
>
> (Isaiah 35:1-2)

> "The majesty of Lebanon shall come to you -
> juniper *(brosh)*, maple *(tidhar)* and cypress *(te'ashur)* trees together."
>
> (Isaiah 60:13)

The desert's place in Jewish tradition is very special. It is important to point out that "desert" *(midbar* in Hebrew) and "wilderness" *(arava* in Hebrew) are not synonyms. The wilderness - *arava* - appears several times in the Bible as a name for various places in the Afro-Syrian Rift between the Sea of Galilee and Eilat. One striking feature immediately apparent to anyone standing on the mountains overlooking the Rift is that it is characterized by regions covered with vegetation immediately adjacent to totally arid areas. These associated landscape components help explain the Hebrew name, *arava*, which comes from the root meaning to mix. The wilderness in this area is indeed a mixture of arid and green regions, of wide salt flats together with alluvial fans created by runoff water and soil from the hills. These sharp contrasts are apparent in the descriptions of Isaiah. For they are "an example in this world" of what can happen in the "end of days" on a much wider scale. Moreover, if we pay attention to the details of the descriptions we can see a clear system by which the prophet divides the trees into two categories: One category will bring the desert *(midbar)* to life and the other will bring glory to the wilderness *(arava)*. At the head of each of these two categories stands one of the two trees that more than any other symbolized the "majesty of Lebanon" - the cedar and the juniper *(brosh)*.

The "bare hills" will be blessed not only with cedars from Lebanon but also with acacia trees. These shade-giving trees will spread from the wadis descending to the *arava* (wilderness). The forest trees, on the other hand, will come to the *midbar* (desert) from the steep slopes of the mountain chasms descending westward to the Mediterranean Sea. These are primarily represented here by the myrtle and the "oil tree."

Oil tree
Although the identification of the "oil tree" is still in doubt, from what is written in the book of Nehemia (8:15), it is clear that the "oil tree" and the myrtle are among the trees that grew in the mountains of Jerusalem during the period of return from Babylonian exile.

Brosh: juniper?
Although as noted on p.94, the *brosh* has not yet been conclusively identified, it is not unwarranted to translate it as juniper. In any case, it is clearly one of the important trees growing in Lebanon, highly suitable for building and manufacture.

Tidhar: maple?
The *tidhar* has a number of identifications. The Jerusalem Talmud (Ktubot, end of chapter 7) and the Midrash Breshit Raba (15,1) translate *tidhar* as *edra*, while Midrash Tanhuma (Truma 9) translates it as *aspandamon*. These names probably point to the tree now called the Syrian *eder* (*Acer syriacum*, maple) which grows well in Lebanon and is found in Israel only in moist places in the Upper Galilee.

Te'ashur: cypress?
The *te'ashur* has not been incontrovertibly identified as yet (see also p.94). Many believe that because of the Talmudic identification as *shurbina* (Rosh Hashana 23a; Baba Batra 80b), the *te'ashur* is the cypress tree, although it is now often called *brosh* in Hebrew. In Israel it is only a domesticated tree, while in Lebanon it grows wild. Some suggest this identification because the cypress tree grows straight up - (*yashar* in Hebrew) - without branching out, hence the name *te'ashur*.

Bivouac under the oaks
Of the several species of oaks growing in Israel, two are most widespread: the common oak (*Quercus caliprinos*) and the Tabor oak (*Quercus ithaburensis*). Unlike the Tabor oak, the common oak is never bare of leaves, because new leaves develop before the old leaves drop off. These leaves are stiff and hard, and sometimes prickly. This *Quercus caliprinos* is found in all the mountainous regions of the Galilee, Judea,

pp. 123-124

Symbols of Uzziah's reign as described by Isaiah
(see pp. 111-113)
p. 124, right
A new generation of oak leaves bud before the death of the previous generation.
pp. 124 left and p. 123
The terebinth at the height of its glory - the glory before defoliation.

and Samaria. It appears to have been the most common forest tree in mountainous areas in biblical times as well.

Today the Tabor oak (*Quercus ithaburensis*) is found mostly in the lower hills around Nazareth and down into the Jezreel Valley, the hills northeast of the Carmel Range, and in parts of the Golan. In the recent past (in the days of Turkish rule in Israel at the end of the 19th century), the Tabor oak also covered large parts of the Sharon Plain. Clear remnants indicate that this oak once also thrived in the low hills southeast of the Carmel area and in different parts of the Jezreel Valley.

One of the Arab names for the *Quercus ithaburensis* is *mal* or *malul*, which is also the name of the village situated in the center of its greatest distribution, on the slopes of the hills of Nazareth overlooking the Jezreel Valley. This village is called Mahalul in the Jerusalem Talmud (Megila 1,1), and is considered to be the biblical Nahalal (Joshua 19:15, 21:35, Nahalol in Judges 1:30). Identical Hebrew names for the tree and settlements can still be found in this region today in Kibbutz Alonim (Oaks) and Moshav Alonei Abba.

Based on this, Ephraim Hareuveni raised the

Leaves of the Tabor oak
*The leaves of the Tabor oak (*Quercus ithaburensis, nahalol *in Hebrew) are dentated but not sharp like those of the common oak. (Compare to photograph on p.133.)*

The *arava*, which has large tracts of green where acacia and palm trees grow, will be able to cover its arid areas with trees representative of the northern mountains of Lebanon: juniper, maple, and cypress.

It is also interesting to compare these descriptions of the transformation of the arid desert and wilderness with the following description:

> "You shall depart (from exile) in joy
> and be led (home) in peace.
> Mountains and hills shall shout aloud before you,
> And all the trees of the field shall clap hands.
> Instead of the *na'atzutz*, a juniper shall rise;
> Instead of a *sirpad*, a myrtle shall grow.
> These shall stand as a testimony to the Lord,
> As an everlasting sign that shall not perish." (Isaiah 55:12-13)

These mountains and hills that shall welcome the returning exiles are, obviously, the **mountains of Judea**, whose cultivation ceased in all areas from which the inhabitants were exiled. As described by the prophets, Isaiah among them, forest thickets covered the abandoned vineyards. (See *Nature in Our Biblical Heritage*, pp.15-22.) In such a forest, various types of trees and shrubs grow, but the most common is the oak, *Quercus caliprinos*. This tree was identified by Ephraim Hareuveni as the *na'atzutz* mentioned by Isaiah. It creates prickly thickets, especially when it grows anew from stumps buried in the ground, but also from seeds, and in conditions where uncontrolled grazing is permitted. The prophet Isaiah is describing the Lord's miracles that will be witnessed by the returning exiles. Not only will the mountains shout before them in song, and "trees of the field" (those orchard trees that were not destroyed) will clap their hands in joy, but in addition the very climate will change; the dry hills of Judea will gain the longed-for moisture of Lebanon. Suddenly all the thickets of prickly oaks *(na'atzutzim)* will be replaced by the refreshing juniper *(brosh)*. "The majesty of Lebanon" will also be reflected in the quantity of fragrant myrtles. These will cover the banks of the rivers that will replace the dry wadi beds in which the *sirpad* is abundant. The hiker who has been scratched going through thickets of prickly oak on Israel's slopes and has reached the dry wadi bed only to have scratches "burned" by the irritating sap of the *sirpad*, can appreciate the joy of Isaiah's prophecy that in time to come, the juniper will replace the prickly oak and the pleasant myrtle will succeed the overpowering *sirpad, Inula viscosa* (see p. 132).

The intense desire for such events is expressed also in the psalm "to Solomon" that portrays the ideal rule of peace; its details suggest the reign of Solomon. The most vivid example is:

> "There shall be abundance of grain in the land,
> growing in plenty to the tops of the mountains;
> its sheaves shall rustle like Lebanon." (Psalms 72:16)

possibility that the *nahalolim* mentioned by Isaiah in 7:19 (see following) are the Tabor oaks, the *Quercus ithaburensis*. He believed that the word *alon* - oak - covers a number of species (as is customary in modern botanical usage), and that to distinguish between the two most widespread species, the Israelites called the Tabor oak *nahalol*, and the common oak *(Quercus caliprinos)* by the name *na'atzutz* because of its sharp "pins" or "tacks" - *na'atz* in modern Hebrew.

This explanation helps to clarify the terrifying picture drawn by Isaiah for King Uzziah's grandson, Ahaz ben Jotham, king of Judah. When Retzin, king of Aram, and Pekakh ben Remalia, king of Israel, went to war against Jerusalem, Ahaz sent "messengers to Tiglath-pileser, king of Assyria, to say: 'I am your servant and your son! Come and save me from the king of Aram and from the king of Israel who are attacking me.'" (II Kings 16:7) Isaiah saw Retzin and Pekakh as "two smoking wisps of firewood" (Isaiah 7:4), insignificant compared to the far greater danger of inviting Assyria to intervene. For if Assyria were to come from the north, Egypt would come from the south to stop Assyria's advance. The land of Israel would become the stage for the confrontation between the two great superpowers:

> "On that day the Lord will whistle for the fly at the ends of the water channels of Egypt and for the bee from the land of Assyria. They shall all come and alight in the rugged ravines and in the clefts of the rocks, and under all the *na'atzutzim* and all the *nahalolim*.　　(Isaiah 7:18-19)

This picture which Isaiah paints for Ahaz becomes very clear when the identification of the *na'atzutzim* and *nahalolim* is understood. The vast armies of Assyria and Egypt will cover all of Israel, and wherever there is shade in uninhabited areas, army units will encamp. In the south of Israel, they will find shade in the ravines and in the clefts of the rocks; in the central part of the land, wherever there are remnants of oak forests, the *na'atzutz (Quercus caliprinos)*; and in the north of Israel the foreign armies will bivouac wherever there remain Tabor oaks, the *nahalol (Quercus ithaburensis)* to shade them.

The common oak (Quercus caliprinos, na'atzutz in Hebrew) covers the slopes of Israel's mountainous areas.

The branches of the cedars of Lebanon stretch out horizontally from the trunk, one above the other. The hard needles grow out of the branches in small clumps. When even the faintest breeze passes through them, a distinct rustling is heard. As the breeze gets stronger, the rustling gets louder until it becomes a piercing whistle.

Sheaves of wheat also produce a rustling when the wind passes through the field. Before the wheat grains have ripened, the green awns are taut as violin strings and play a song delighting every heart.

> "Rabbi Eleazar [23] and Rabbi Shimon [21] say:...When do the sheaves sing? - in the month of Nissan." (Rosh Hashana 8b)

The delicate song of the sheaves in the Passover month of Nissan (approximately April) gives way to louder and louder music as the kernels ripen and fill with starch in the weeks leading to the wheat harvest in late May or early June. By then the awns are hard, yellow, and breakable; their summer rustling is very different from their spring song. The author of Psalm 72 sees Israel blessed in "the end of days" with grain growing not only in the broad fields of the plain but also up the slopes to the mountain tops. But this is not all. The grain will grow to such size that the sound of the rustling sheaves will be as loud as the wind passing through the tall and majestic cedars of Lebanon.

It is appropriate to close this book with a midrash that marvels at prophesied abundance in the Messianic Age - the "end of days" - when even wheat will be the size of trees.

> "Our Sages said: 'There shall be abundance of grain in the land, growing in plenty to the tops of the mountains.' (Psalms 72:16) This means that wheat shall grow as tall as a date palm and grow even on the mountain tops. But will it not be difficult to harvest this grain? The Bible says, 'Its sheaves shall rustle like Lebanon.' The Lord, Blessed be He, will bring a wind from His storehouse and blow upon the wheat, which will then drop its kernels, and a man will go out into the field and bring in handfuls and this will suffice as livelihood for him and his family." (Ktubot, 111b)

"The trees of the field...clap their hands."
In biblical terminology, "the trees of the field" are usually cultivated fruit trees : "The trees of the field shall yield their fruit and the land shall yield its produce." (Ezekiel 34:27)

> "When you are at war, and lay siege to a city for a long time in order to take it, do not destroy its trees by taking an axe to them; you may eat of them, but you shall not cut them down. For are the trees of the field human that they may seek refuge from your siege? Only those trees that you know are not fruit trees may you cut down and use in siege works against the city that is at war with you, until it falls." (Deuteronomy 20:19-20)

In these words the Bible differentiates between the "trees of the field" (fruit trees, whose destruction was forbidden even for building siege works) and trees that were not planted by man. Permission to cut down nonfruit trees only "until it (the city) falls" may be seen as a commandment not to denude the area of wild trees after the city has fallen, for then the survivors will need the wood for fuel and building material.

This moving view of the trees of the field is

expressed by the rhetorical question: "For are the trees of the field human that they may seek refuge from your siege?" A farmer may have fled to a fortified town, leaving to the mercy of the besieging enemy the fruit trees that he had planted and cultivated for years. Unlike the man, the tree can neither escape nor defend itself. The soldier who becomes absolute master of the tree's fate is therefore commanded to spare the tree. This injunction, of course, also relates to the need to settle and cultivate the land so that it will survive as a fruitful country and not be turned into a wasteland because of war - an example of environmental protection even in time of war!

The same spirit pervades the words of Rabbi Eliezer ben Hyrcanus [13], who was a farmer in his youth: "When a fruit tree is chopped down, its cry carries from one end of the earth to the other, but it is not heard." (Pirkei De-Rabbi Eliezer Hagadol 34,19) The trees of the field that "clap their hands" with joy in greeting the returning exiles are also "motivated" by the same concept: joy at the return of those who nurtured them and the removal of the danger that an enemy might raise an axe to them again.

This attitude towards the tree and the resettlement of Israel is also affirmed in the words of Rabban Johanan ben Zakkai [10]: "If you have a sapling in your hand and you are told, 'The Messiah has come!' first plant the sapling and then go to greet him." (Avot De Rabbi Natan, 31) Rabban Johanan ben Zakkai was the Sage who, even before the destruction of the Second Temple in 70 CE, created in Yavne a center that would continue the dynasty of spiritual leaders for the nation after the destruction he foresaw. Ben Zakkai's "practical Zionism" enables us to understand his unequivocal instruction. If you first insure life for the sapling in your hands, this will be a more fitting welcome than if you go out to greet the Messiah and let the sapling wither. For in Jewish tradition the coming of the Messiah is unconditionally bound up with the settlement of the Land of Israel. Thus, if you first plant the sapling and then go to greet the Messiah, you will have accomplished two good deeds that complement each other!

"(Israel) may flower like the lily."
The Lilium candidum *L. is a refreshing beauty on shaded, dew-nourished slopes.*

Appendix of Terms and Names

1. Authorities differ on the etymology and meaning of the word **Mishna**. Some think it is related to the word *shnaim*, two, and expresses the idea that the Mishna ranks second to the Bible. Others connect it with the verb *shan'e*, meaning to teach, teach orally, repeat, learn by heart. According to this derivation the word *mishna* would indicate that its teachings were transmitted orally through the generations, in contradistinction to the "written Law" of the Pentateuch - the **Torah** - which is designated in Hebrew also as *Mikra*, that which is read.

The Mishna was first arranged in six principal divisions (*s'darim* - orders) by Hillel [8]; this system was further improved upon by Rabbi Akiva [16] and subsequently by Rabbi Meir [27]. Finally Rabbi Judah Ha-Nasi [28] completed the work of redaction towards the end of the second century CE.

Since the Mishna was at first transmitted orally and thus had to be committed to memory, it is not surprising that the style of such a vast volume of material is very concise - so much so that the Mishnaic text would, in many instances, be almost impossible to understand without the vast commentary which is called Gemara.

The **Tosefta** is an "appendix" or "supplement" to the Mishna, dating from the fifth or sixth centuries CE. It contains many *halakhot* [2], maxims, and decisions frequently quoted in the Gemara.

The name Talmud originally referred to the **Gemara** alone. It was only in later times that Talmud came to be applied to both the Mishna and the Gemara as a combined work. The Mishna forms the older portion of the Talmud. The word Talmud literally means study, and it embodies the opinions, teachings and mental labors of the ancient Jewish scholars to expound and develop the religious and civil laws of the Bible during a period of some eight centuries, from 300 BCE to 500 CE. The Talmud includes two distinct elements, *halakha* and *aggada* [3].

There are two compilations of the Gemara: the **Babylonian Talmud** and the **Jerusalem** (or Palestinian) **Talmud**, differing from each other in language and content. The former was compiled in Babylon (in the Academies of Nehardea, Sura and Pumbedita) and the latter in the Academies flourishing in Israel (Tiberias, Sepphoris and Caesarea). The Babylonian Talmud is fuller; its style is less difficult, and its discussions are more thorough and detailed; it has therefore been accepted as authoritative on most matters except laws relating to the Land of Israel.

(Paraphrased from Blackman, Philip, *General Introduction to the Mishnah*, Judaica Press, New York, 1964.)

2. *halakha*, plural *halakhot*: literally "law"; the generic term for the entire legal system of Judaism, including all the detailed laws and observances that govern daily Jewish life.

3. *aggada*: literally, narrative; homilies not intended as authoritative legal explanations but rather as devices for learning through association by expounding on words in the Bible by means of humor, satire, fantasy, and exaggerated storytelling.

4. *midrash*, plural *midrashim*: the designation of a particular genre of rabbinic literature constituting an anthology of homilies, consisting of both biblical exegesis and sermons, forming a running commentary on specific books of the Bible.

5. **Sages**: the spiritual-religious leaders and teachers of the Jewish people for a thousand years, from the time of the rebuilding of the Second Temple (530 BCE) to the completion of the Babylonian Talmud in the late fifth century CE. The Sages of the Mishna and Gemara (collectively the Talmudic Sages) formulated and set down the legal system of Judaism. A large portion of the Talmud comprises the homilies and stories that the Sages created as a further means of explaining each chapter, verse, and sometimes even a single word of the Bible.

6. *tanna*, plural *tannaim*: those Sages mentioned in the Mishna or of the Mishnaic period, i.e., from about 20 CE to the final redaction of the Oral Law (the Mishna) circa 200 CE by Rabbi Judah Ha-Nasi [28]. These two centuries are generally divided into five generations, a useful frame of reference that has been used since it was first introduced in the second half of the twelfth century. The title **rabbi** or **rabban** is given to all the *tannaim*.

7. **Sanhedrin**: the supreme political, religious and judicial body in Israel during the Roman period, both before and after the destruction of the Second Temple, until about 425 CE.

8. **Hillel** and **Shammai**: two giants of the Second Temple period, who lived at the end of the first century BCE and the beginning of the first century CE. They founded two schools of exposition of the Oral Law. Mishnaic tradition holds that the School of Shammai chose the stricter, more conservative legal viewpoints (halakhic rulings), while the School of Hillel was more lenient in its *halakhot*. After the destruction of the Temple in 70 CE, the rulings of the School of Hillel gained ascendancy in almost all matters, so that, as a general rule, the Mishna and the Gemara follow the School of Hillel.

9. **Rabban Gamaliel Ha-Zaken** ("the elder"): first half of first century CE, first generation of *tannaim*; grandson of Hillel; *nasi* (head) of the Sanhedrin and leader of the Jewish people until the destruction of the Second Temple in 70 CE. The Sages' regard for him was expressed in their saying: "When Rabban Gamaliel the elder died, the glory of the Torah ceased, and purity and saintliness perished." (Sota 9:15)

10. **Rabban Johanan ben Zakkai**: first century CE; according to tradition, the youngest of Hillel's pupils and his spiritual heir. Foreseeing the destruction of the Second Temple, he established the Academy of Yavne. When he died, the Mishna states that "the luster of wisdom ceased." (Sota 9:15)

11. **Rabban Simeon ben Gamaliel I**: first century CE; son of Rabban Gamaliel Ha-Zaken; *nasi* of the Sanhedrin in the generation of the destruction of the Second Temple; killed by the Romans.

12. **Rabban Gamaliel of Yavne**: second generation of *tannaim* (80-110); grandson of Rabban Gamaliel the elder; *nasi* of the Sanhedrin in Yavne for some 30 years after the destruction of the Temple. He was not only the chief religious authority of his time but also the accepted national-political leader, recognized by the Roman government as spokesman for the Jews.

13. **Rabbi Eliezer ben Hyrcanus**: second generation of *tannaim* (80-110); the first and most important of Rabban Johanan ben Zakkai's students; hundreds of *halakhot* are recorded in his name; (he is sometimes referred to simply as "Rabbi Eliezer" or as "Rabbi Eliezer the Great.") According to *aggada*, he was a farmer in his youth and began his studies at a relatively

late age. He was the head of the Academy of Lod in Israel; brother-in-law of Rabban Gamaliel of Yavne; teacher of Rabbi Akiva.

14. Rabbi Tarfon: second (80-110) and third (110-135) generation of *tannaim*; one of the leading Sages of Yavne, called "the father of all Israel;" of a priestly family; in his childhood, he had seen the Holy Temple in its full glory. Rabbi Judah bar Ilai was one of his disciples, as was Rabbi Akiva.

15. Rabbi Eleazar ben Azariah: second (80-110) and third (110-135) generation of *tannaim*; when Rabban Gamaliel of Yavne was dismissed as head of the Academy, Rabbi Eleazar ben Azaria was appointed to replace him.

16. Rabbi Akiva: (c. 50-135 CE) considered the greatest of all Mishanic Sages, belonging to the third generation of *tannaim* (110-135); Rabbi Akiva was active between the destruction of the Second Temple and the Bar Kokhba revolt against Rome (132-135). Judah Ha-Nasi's *Mishna Codex* is drawn largely on the views and rulings of Akiva. He was a shepherd for 40 years and began his study of the Torah late in life. At the age of 85, he was tortured to death by the Romans for openly teaching the Bible in defiance of the Emperor Hadrian's edict. His last 5 disciples were Rabbi Meir, Rabbi Judah bar Ilai, Rabbi Yose ben Halafta, Rabbi Simeon bar Yohai, and Rabbi Eleazar ben Shammua, the leading lights of the fourth generation of *tannaim*. They disseminated the study of Torah in Israel after the destruction wreaked by the Roman occupiers following the failure of the Bar Kokhba revolt.

17. Rabbi Judah ben Bathyra: third generation of *tannaim* (110-135); born in Rome, established an academy in Nisibis in Babylon which was among those centers of study the Sages advised students to attend. He was regarded as an authority of equal rank to Rabbi Akiva who was a friend and associate.

18. Abba Saul: *tanna* of the third (110-135) and fourth (135-170) generations; he was a grave digger by profession; transmitted traditions with regard to the pathology and growth of the human embryo, as well as the structure and utensils of the Temple.

19. Rabban Simeon ben Gamaliel II: fourth generation of *tannaim* (135-170); son of Rabban Gamaliel of Yavne, father of Judah Ha-Nasi; in his youth he fled to Babylon to escape Roman persecution in the wake of the Bar Kokhba revolt; when the edicts were removed, he returned to Israel to head the Usha Academy and serve as *nasi* of the Sanhedrin. His authority is reflected in the rule of Rabbi Johanan: "Wherever Simeon ben Gamaliel taught in our Mishna, the *halakha* follows." (Ketuba 77a)

20. Rabbi Joshua ben Korha: fourth generation of *tannaim* (135-170); his forte was *aggada*; known for his debates with gentiles on matters of faith and religion.

21. Rabbi Shimon (Simeon) **(bar Yohai):** fourth generation of *tannaim* (135-170); pupil of Rabbi Akiva; escaped the death sentence imposed by Rome by hiding out in a cave with his son, Eleazar, for 13 (some sources say 12) years, where they lived off carob fruit and water from a spring which miraculously appeared at the cave entrance. The basic work of Kabbalistic literature, the *Zohar*, is attributed to him.

22. Rabbi Jacob bar Korshai: fourth generation of *tannaim* (135-170); Rabbi Judah Ha-Nasi was his student.

23. Rabbi Eleazar ben Shammua: fourth generation of *tannaim* (135-170); disciple of Rabbi Akiva; one of his sayings is "Living in the Land of Israel is equivalent to all the *mitzvot* (good deeds) of the Bible." (Sifri Re'e 80)

24. Rabbi Hananiah ben Gamaliel: brother of Rabban Simeon ben Gamliel; apparently a disciple of Rabbi Tarfon.

25. Rabbi Judah (bar Ilai): one of the greatest *tannaim* in the fourth generation (135-170); one of Rabbi Akiva's disciples; earlier he served Rabbi Tarfon. He was the halakhic authority in the house of Simeon ben Gamaliel III; Judah Ha-Nasi was one of his pupils.

26. Rabbi Nehemiah: fourth generation of *tannaim* (135-170); worked as a potter; laid the foundations for the composition of the Tosefta; one of Rabbi Akiva's last pupils.

27. Rabbi Meir: considered the greatest *tanna* of the fourth generation (135-170) and one of the leaders of the post-Bar Kokhba generation; the most famous of Rabbi Akiva's disciples; played a decisive part in the development of the Mishna, laying the foundation for the Mishna of Judah Ha-Nasi. His wife, **Beruryah**, was a scholar who participated in discussions on halakhic rulings with the Sages of her generation, and several rulings are given in her name.

28. Rabbi Judah Ha-Nasi (Rabbi or Rabbeni Ha-Kadosh, "our holy teacher"): son of Rabban Simeon ben Gamaliel II; leading light of the fifth generation of *tannaim* (170-200); *nasi* of the Sanhedrin and redactor of the Mishna. According to aggadic tradition, he was born on the day of Rabbi Akiva's death.

29. Rabban Gamaliel III: eldest son of Rabbi Judah Ha-Nasi; served as *nasi* of the Sanhedrin after his father's death; belongs to the transitional generation between the *tannaim* and the *amoraim* [31].

30. Rabbi Simeon bar Rabbi: (first half of the 3rd c.) the youngest son of Rabbi Judah Ha-Nasi; considered to have played a significant part in arranging and completing the Mishna undertaken by his father.

31. *amora*, plural *amoraim*: Those Sages mentioned in the Gemara or active from the early third century (when the Mishna was codified) until the completion of the Babylonian Talmud at the end of the fifth century CE. It is customary to divide the amoraic period into eight generations, although many of the scholars span two successive generations. The first five generations consist of both Palestinian and Babylonian *amoraim*. The last three generations however, are limited to Babylonian *amoraim*, since the Jerusalem Talmud was completed about a century before the Babylonian. The title **rabbi** or **rabban** was given not only to all the *tannaim*, but also to those *amoraim* **who resided in Israel. Rav or the absence of a title before the name indicates *amoraim* of the Babylonian Talmud.**

32. Rabbi Oshaiah (Hoshaiah): one of the greatest Sages in Israel during the first generation of *amoraim* (220-250).

33. Rabbi Jonathan (ben Elazar): *amora* in Israel of the first generation (220-250); considered one of the greatest aggadists.

34. Rabbi Joshua ben Levi: first generation *amora* (220-250); head of the Academy at Lod in Israel; although a halakhist whose opinions were always accepted, he was especially renowned as an aggadist, and was himself the hero of an *aggada* which narrates that he was worthy of and achieved the revelation of Elijah the Prophet.

35. Rav (Rabbi Abba bar Aivo; also called "Abba the Tall"): the first of the Babylonian *amoraim*; he was a pupil of Rabbi Judah Ha-Nasi and founded the Academy of Sura.

36. Rav Judah (bar Ezekiel): one of the greatest Babylonian *amoraim* of the second generation (250-290); founder of the Academy of Pumbedita in Babylon. According to tradition, was born on the day Rabbi Judah Ha-Nasi died. One of the first pupils of Rav, he transmitted hundreds of Rav's sayings.

37. Rabbi Johanan ben Nappaha ("son of the blacksmith"): the greatest of the *amoraim* in Israel in the second generation (250-290); his father died when he was conceived, his mother died in childbirth; all ten of his children predeceased him. Rabbi Johanan sold all his possessions in order to study Torah; founded the Academy of Tiberias. He was a pupil of Rabbi Oshaiah in Kisrin and the teacher of Rabbi Abbahu. Rambam [62] and others credit him with the compilation of the Jerusaelm Talmud even though it was completed almost 100 years after his death.

38. Reish Lakish (Rabbi Simeon ben-Lakish): one of the greatest *amoraim* of Israel in the second generation (250-290); head of the Academy at Tiberias together with Rabbi Johanan. He was a gladiator in his youth. He was so highly esteemed for his personal integrity that if he was seen talking to anyone in public, that person would be lent money without any witnesses.

39. Rabbi Hama bar Hanina: *amora* of Israel in the second generation (250-290); distinguished as an aggadist; lived in Tzipori in the Galilee.

40. Rabbi Samuel bar Nahmani: *amora* of Israel in the second (250-290) and third (290-320) generation; student of Rabbi Jonathan; he resided in Lod; known as one of the great aggadists of his time.

41. Rabbi Abba bar Kahana: famous orator and one of the greatest exponents of *aggada* in the third generation of *amoraim* in Israel (290-320).

42. Rav Hisda: Babylonian *amora*, one of the greatest Sages of the second (250-290) and third (290-320) generations; one of the most frequently quoted scholars in the Jerusalem and Babylonian Talmuds, both in *halakha* and *aggada*. He rebuilt in his own cost the Sura Academy which had fallen into disrepair. His early years were spent in poverty but he became rich as a brewer.

43. Rabbi Abbahu: *amora* in Israel in the third generation (290-320); head of the Kisrin Academy and *bet din* (judicial court). He was learned in mathematics, rhetoric, and Greek, which he taught his daughters. He was held in high esteem by the Roman authorities who regarded him as a spokesman for his people and "showed favor to his generation for his sake."

44. Rabbi Isaac bar Tavlai: *amora* in Israel in the third generation (290-320).

45. Rabbi Ze'eira: one of the greatest halakhic Sages in Israel during the third generation of *amoraim* (290-320); he came to Israel from Babylon and joined the Academy at Tiberias. His name is one of the most frequently mentioned in the Babylonian and Jerusalem Talmuds; hundreds of dicta in his name are transmitted by many different Sages.

46. Rav Hananiah "Friend of the Sages": Babylonian *amora* of the third generation (290-320) who moved to Israel.

47. Rabbah bar bar Hana: *amora* of the third generation (290-320); pupil of Rabbi Johanan Nappaha; born in Babylon, came to Israel to study Torah, and traveled in many lands. He achieved great renown for his remarkable legends (known as the "*aggadot* of Rabbah bar bar Hana") of his journeys by sea and land.

48. Rabbi Samuel bar Rav Isaac: *amora* of Israel of the third generation (290-320), whose main fame is as an aggadist.

49. Rav Dimai (Dimi): Babylonian *amora* of the third (290-320) and fourth (320-350) generations, who traveled to Israel from time to time and transmitted to the academies in Babylon the sayings and *halakhot* of the Israel Sages. From this comes the expression in the Talmud: "When Rav Dimai came, he said..."

50. Rabbi Judah bar Simeon (Sima): *amora* from Israel of the third (290-320) and fourth (320-350) generations; famous aggadist.

51. Rabbi Levi bar Hiya (bar Hita): aggadist in the fourth generation (320-350) of *amoraim* in Israel.

52. Rabbi Huna (bar Avin the Cohen): *amora* in Israel of the fourth generation (320-350); came to Israel from Babylon to study in Tiberias; frequently mentioned in the Jerusalem Talmud; accepted as an authority in practical *halakhot*.

53. Rav Nahman ben Isaac: one of the great *amoraim* in Babylon of the fourth generation (320-350); frequently quoted in the Babylonian Talmud; joined the Academy of Pumbedita.

54. Rabbi Azariah: *amora* from Israel of the fifth and last generation (350-375); transmitted numerous aggadatic sayings, many in the name of Rabbi Judah bar Simeon and Rabbi Joshua ben Levi.

55. Rav Papa: one of the great Babylonian *amoraim* in the fifth generation (350-375); he was a wealthy businessman, an expert brewer of date beer and sold poppy seeds. Founder and head of the Academy of Naresh (near Sura) which was famous for the number of its pupils; considered one of the editors of the Talmud.

56. Rabbi Tanhuma bar Abba: *amora* in Israel of the fifth generation (350-375); compiler of *Midrash Tanhuma*; one of the most prolific aggadists; distinguished for his defense of Jews and Judaism against non-Jews.

57. Ameimar: Babylonian *amora* of the fifth (350-375) and sixth (375-425) generations; considered one of the leading Sages of Nehardea.

58. Rav Huna bar Natan: Babylonian *amora* of the fifth (350-375) and sixth (375-425) generations; exilarch in the days of Rav Ashi; studied with Ameimar in the Academy of Nehardea.

59. Rav Ashi (Rabbana): greatest Babylonian *amora* of the sixth (375-425) generation; redactor of the Babylonian Talmud; for 60 years served as head of the Academy of Sura; his contemporaries said of him, "Never since the days Rabbi Judah Ha-Nasi were learning and greatness combined in one person as they were in Rav Ashi."

60. Rashi (Rabbi Shlomo Yitzhaki): lived in France and Germany in the 11th century. The most popular and authoritative commentator of all ages on the Bible and Talmud, his works became the bases for most later traditional biblical and Talmudic commentaries.

61. Ibn Ezra: twelfth century Spain, most widely studied biblical commentator after Rashi.

62. Rambam (Rabbi Moses ben-Maimon): b.1135 in Cordoba, Spain, d.1204 in Israel; rabbinic authority, codifier, philosopher and physician. Considered the most illustrious figure in Judaism of the post-Talmudic era and one of the greatest Jewish luminaries of all time. Rambam's two great works are the *Mishne Torah*, a systematic classification by subject matter of the entire Talmudic and post-Talmudic halakhic literature, and the *Guide for the Perplexed*, a philosophical interpretation of the Bible. The latter is not only one of the most important Jewish philosophical works of all time, but one which exercised a profound influence on medieval Christian scholastic thought, especially that of Albertus Magnus, Thomas Aquinas and Duns Scotus.

63. Radak (Rabbi David Kimkhi): 1160-1235?, Provence, France; one of the outstanding biblical commentators who strove for clarity and readability in his exegesis.

64. Kabbala: Jewish mysticism, which seeks apprehension of God and creation beyond the bounds of intellect alone and sees in nature not only the hand of God, but one of the main paths leading to awareness of Him. After the expulsion of Jews from Spain in 1492, the center of Kabbalism moved to Safed in Israel, whence its influence spread to many of the other mainstreams of Jewish and Christian thought.

---

p. 133

Oaks in the hills of Jerusalem
With the right conditions, even the common oak (Quercus caliprinos, na'atzutz) can reach great height in Israel.

pp. 134-135

top to bottom
The myrtle's look-alike
According to Dr. Ephraim Hareuveni, the sirpad is the plant Inula viscosa, known in Israel by its Arabic name, tayun. This shrub is well known for its irritating sap. It is widespread along dry river beds and banks. From afar, clumps of this tayun look like thickets of myrtle bushes, not only in size, shape, and color, but also in the growth pattern of its branches.
right
Flowering myrtle branch

Indices

to *Tree and Shrub in Our Biblical Heritage*

Numbers followed by ★ indicate narrow-columned text. Numbers followed by □ indicate mention within citations. Numbers in ( ) indicate photographs and illustrations.

Acacia trees in the Arava Valley against the background of the mountains near Eilat.

INDEX TO BOOKS OF THE BIBLE

INDEX TO NAMES AND PLACE NAMES

Indices

to *Nature in Our Biblical Heritage*

Numbers followed by ★ indicate narrow-columned text. Numbers followed by □ indicate mention within citations. Numbers in ( ) indicate photographs and illustrations.

INDEX TO PLANT NAMES

Indices to *Nature in Our Biblical Heritage*

INDEX TO NAMES AND PLACE NAMES